DOMESTICALLY CHALLENGED

A Working Mom's

Survival Guide to Becoming

a Stay-at-Home Mom

alana morales

Domestically Challenged: A Working Mom's Survival Guide to Becoming a Stay-at-Home Mom

by Alana Morales

Published by The Mom-Writers Publishing Cooperative
Wyatt-MacKenzie Publishing, Inc., Deadwood, OR
www.WyMacPublishing.com (541) 964-3314

Requests for permission or further information should be
addressed to: Wyatt-MacKenzie Publishing,
15115 Highway 36, Deadwood, Oregon 97430

Printed in the United States of America

DOMESTICALLY CHALLENGED

*A Working Mom's
Survival Guide to Becoming
a Stay-at-Home Mom*

by alana morales

Dedication

*In loving memory of my grandfather
Richard Frye, who was a symbol of dedication
and hard work.*

Thank you for the lessons you taught me.

I love you and miss you dearly.

TABLE OF CONTENTS

SECTION 3

The Logistics Of It All

SECTION 4
It's All About You!

Foreword

"Mommy! Mommy!" screamed 4 year old Heather. "Mommy, Mommy, Mommy!" echoed 8 year old Justin. "Mommy, Mommy, Mommy, Mommy!" they both chimed at the top of their lungs. "Don't call me Mommy!" I cried at the top of my lungs. "Mommy doesn't live here anymore. " And with that, I collapsed onto the floor in total motherhood exhaustion.

"If we don't call you Mommy, what are we supposed to call you?" Justin questioned. "And if you don't live here anymore, are you going to go live with the animals in the barn?" intoned Heather. In an instant my two shrieking children metamorphosed into the two most compassionate caring angels a mother could imagine. They were really concerned with discovering a new name for me as well as finding a comfortable safe place where I could live closeby. For at least five minutes they debated this unusual scenario. "Should we call her 'Cynthia' or 'Nonie's Girl' or 'Miss? She *could* live in the barn if the hay is clean. We like it there. Or maybe the shed? No, too crowded with tools. I think the bird aviary would be too cramped, don't you?' Of course, I started laughing, hugged them both, and let them know I'd be staying right here inside our house.

Can you relate? Being a mom is a tough assignment yet the most important job in the world. No matter what our position was in the world of work outside the home, our title of Mommy is the most challenging. With humor and grace, Alana Morales has come to the rescue of all of us who erroneously thought we could be Superwoman. With her book, *Domestically Challenged, a Working Mom's Survival Guide to Becoming a Stay-at-Home Mom*, Alana offers simple straight-forward tips that help every mom transition from the workplace to home base.

This survival guide supplies information on everything from how to communicate better with your mate to how to manage the family schedule without losing your mind. Alana gives us permission to take a personal time-out for rest, relaxation, and rejuvenation without guilt. If you are not a great cook or perfect housekeeper, no problem. Remember you are home to nurture your children, not to become June Cleaver. Tips include how to encourage your children to get involved with the cooking, cleaning, and chores. If you want to start a home based business or work part time, you'll find suggestions for stretching your mind as well as your pocketbook.

In order to drive a car, we have to take lessons, practice, and pass a test. With parenting it's a Yoda thing — "Do, or do not. There is no try!" Children don't come with manuals as new cars do. Parenting means taking the leap and learning to fly. Domestically Challenged is the safety net helping moms build confidence, have fun, and leave the worrying for someone else.

In my experience as Mommy, I have found that by giving my children age appropriate responsibilities, I have been rewarded with kids who appreciate life without feeling entitled. When I am playful, organized, and focused, they mirror my behavior to make my job more fun. It's a joy to be creative and spontaneous, however recognizing that our children are not just "mini me's".

Enjoy *Domestically Challenged*. Keep it with you at all times. It is a like having a support team with a personal parenting coach. If Alana had written this book when I was raising my kids, I probably would have responded more positively to my Mommy incident. Of course, memories are made of moments like those. As predicted, I do indeed spend quite a number of my waking hours in our barn and my children did re-name me. I am known as Momma Bear and proud of it. Hear me roar!

~ Cynthia Brian, home, garden, and parenting expert
at ClubMom, author of *Be the Star You Are!*

©2006 Cynthia Brian, Starstyle® Productions, LLC. *Cynthia Brian, wife, mother, chief cook and bottle washer, is a popular speaker, dynamic writer, and savvy media personality appearing regularly on radio, TV, and in print. Besides hosting a radio program with her daughter, she is the New York Times best selling author of* **Chicken Soup for the Gardener's Soul** *, author of* **Be the Star You Are!®**, **The Business of Show Business**, *and* **Miracle Moments®**. *The charity, Be the Star You Are!, a 501 c3 was founded by Cynthia to empower women, families, and youth through improved literacy and positive messages.* (www.bethestaryouare.org) *When she's not writing, coaching or performing, you'll find her in the barnyard with her children! cynthia@star-style.com, www.star-style.com*

SECTION 1
In The Beginning...

Chapter 1:
Becoming a Stay at Home Mom

Chapter 2:
The Myth of the Supermom

Chapter 3:
Dealing with Husbands

Chapter 1:
Me, A Stay At Home Mom?

Like most personal journeys in life, my path to becoming a stay at home mom (SAHM) was not exactly a straight line. In fact, I was one of those working moms who always looked at SAHM's with a bit of contempt. In my mind, a SAHM was a mom who simply couldn't handle the stress of working and raising children as well as I could. Smug? Sure. Ignorant? I didn't think so at the time.

Then I had my daughter.

I remember my "moment of clarity" very well. You see, in my working life I was a teacher and by the time my daughter was approaching the three month old mark, I had been preparing for my return to the classroom for several weeks already. I was going to do it all, be it all and juggle it all with amazing grace and style. Perfect timing for an epiphany, wouldn't you say? It came in the form of my darling daughter as she was waking up from her nap, full of smiles.

My husband, the lucky dog, was preparing for an out of town bachelor party camping trip.

I leaned over to pick my daughter up from her crib, took one look at her gummy smile and burst into tears. My husband, surely envisioning his bachelor bash sliding down the drain, hurried into the room.

"What happened? Is she ok?" he asked.

"She's fine" I sobbed.

"Well, then what's wrong?" my husband asked, his face full of incredulity.

"Look at her smile." I stammered.

"Um, yeah. It's real – cute?" he replied. At this point, he really had no idea what was going on.

"I know." More blubbering.

"What's wrong?" he tried again.

"Well, if I go back to work I am going to miss all those smiles and she is so beautiful and her brother has so much fun with her and those are *my* smiles and if I go back to work and put her in childcare then someone else will be getting *my* smiles."

My husband's stare was blank, but I'm fairly certain his two most prevalent thoughts were "Her hormones are even more out of whack than I thought" and "Thank goodness I am going to be gone for three days."

I freely admit that I was surprised by my feelings too. I had never, *ever*, thought about being a SAHM and laughed hysterically whenever one of my friends would ask me if it was an option I was considering. *Stay home? Just because I had a baby? Are you crazy?* I *liked* being a working mom. I *liked* having a career and a family and *I really liked* that I could juggle it all. But at that moment, looking into her tiny, angelic face, I realized that I *loved* my kids too much to leave them and that I would do whatever it took to be home with them.

By the time my husband had returned from his trip I had figured out every possible budget issue he might put forth and even had plans for how I could bring in some side money if necessary. I had complete answers, in essay form practically, to every other conceivable objection he might have. In the end, we both knew that while it was a purely emotional decision, it was also a purely *right* decision.

Three days later I put in for my extended leave from teaching and never went back.

Your path to being at home may not have been so shocking to you. Maybe you:

- Always knew you wanted to be at home.
- Didn't know you wanted to be home until you had your first child. Then it just made sense.
- Looked at the costs of childcare and realized it wasn't worth it financially to work outside the home. Most couples are shocked to discover they can actually save money by giving up one salary, thereby giving up daycare, babysitting, etc.
- Missed another program or teacher conference due to your work schedule and decided to reprioritize — after all, your children are only young once.
- Were laid off from your job and decided that you could find a way to make staying at home work.

Whatever the case, you are home now and that's what matters. The funny thing is that staying at home is nothing like you will have imagined it. Yeah, you get to do all the fun kid stuff just like you did when you played hooky from work to spend time with your children, but it is the behind-the-scenes action that will take you by surprise. It is nonstop, draining, demanding, fabulous, frustrating, joyous and jumbled — everything that is invisible to the outside world — to anyone who has not done it. Quite simply, never will you have imagined that being a SAHM is the hardest job in the world.

I worked as an office manager until my son was 14 months old. Then my family moved because my husband graduated college and received a wonderful job offer in a different state. At a cocktail party given by my husband's company a few weeks after we had moved, introductions were being made and everyone was telling what they did. I stated that I was a stay-at-home mom and got incredulous looks from the other women in the group. One of them asked, "Aren't you bored? What do you do all day, watch soap operas?"

Obviously this woman had never spent much time with a 14-month old.

-Julie G., Utah

6 Things Nobody Told You About Being a SAHM

1. Staying home all the time is much more difficult than working. There are no doors to hide behind when you need quiet or have a deadline to meet.

2. Your kids will not magically behave like angels all the time just because you are home with them. If anything, they will sprout horns and tails as their comfort level with you increases.

3. Your house will not always be clean because you are home all the time. Learn this now: Dust will wait, the kids will not.

4. You will not necessarily have time to cook wonderful five course meals every day now that you are home. You will, however, perfect the art of Macaroni & Cheese and microwaved hot dogs.

5. Being at home all the time will occasionally get boring, frustrating and stressful — sometimes all at the same time — you are dealing with people who have the attention span of gnats and who feel it is their right to watch you go to the bathroom.

6. Even though you are now "at home" you may not be home all that much. The "S" in SAHM certainly does not stand for "stuck". Park, playground, playgroup, errands, soccer, swimming, everything, everywhere, all at the same time. You are magic.

You might not like hearing these things, but while the truth is not always what you want to hear, it is what you need to hear, and as a fellow SAHM who had no idea what she was getting herself into, I feel it is my responsibility (and perverse pleasure) to enlighten you.

Staying home all the time is much more difficult than working.

Like it or not, being home is a tough job for several reasons. One, you will be around your kids constantly. This is a double edged sword. Two, you don't get scheduled lunch breaks where you can read a book or run errands. Count yourself lucky when you get to eat the bread crusts from their sandwiches. Three, you will be around your kids constantly. (A point worth repeating.) Four, you can forget vacation time, comp time or even "you" time. Depending on the age of your kids, you will be lucky to get potty time — it will be up to you to take 'me' time; no one is going to offer it to you, no matter how dark the circles under your eyes are or how evil the glint is inside them.

When you are home there aren't any office politics or deadline crises to worry about. This is good because you don't have the mental energy to waste on such mundane tasks; however, the downside is that you aren't engaging your brain with such mundane tasks. You will have to put more effort into finding ways to use your brain on an adult level. And for the record, mocking the morning cartoons does not count as mental exercise.

Your kids will not magically behave like angels all the time because you are home.

Another common myth about being a SAHM is that when you stay home, your constant presence will ensure that your kids will always act wonderfully since you are on hand to redirect their behavior and such. Yeah, right. And owning a treadmill ensures that you don't gain weight. I hate to break it to you, but it all takes effort, so be prepared. Remember when your kids acted really, really good for the babysitter and then acted like a monster for you after work? Well, now you are taking the babysitter out of the equation.

Kids will be kids and you being home with them will not change that. In fact, as their comfort level with you increases, so does their security level, meaning they will feel less at risk and freer to fully express themselves. They will talk back more. They will fight with their siblings more. They will throw monstrous temper tantrums more. Now, instead of only having to deal with them after a long day of work, the joy of their personalities (whether good or bad) will be yours to savor 24 hours a day.

Your house will not always be clean because you are home all the time.

When I first began staying home, I couldn't believe how messy my house was. It wasn't until I thought about it that it made sense. When you stay home, you are, well, *home* a lot more. Instead of making a mess in the four hours between arriving home from work and bedtime you can now make a mess all day long.

This is an incredibly frustrating reality for new SAHM's, but remember, you are home to be with your kids, not to have a model home. Despite what it initially feels like, you will find balance and the messiness will even out. It might take a while depending on how old your kids are, but you will eventually make peace with a certain level of filth.

You will not necessarily have time to cook wonderful five course meals every day now that you are home.

If you were used to getting take out a few nights a week while you were working, it can be a difficult habit to break. If you don't enjoy cooking, it will be even harder. Just because you are home does not mean you will be serving up meals like Emeril (and if you are, feel free to share your address with me). It's ok if you have to learn how to cook — having ovaries does not automatically make you Betty Crocker. As long as you are making an attempt and the family can eat your attempts on a semi-regular basis you are making progress.

Being at home all the time will occasionally get boring, frustrating and stressful — sometimes all at the same time.

When you first begin staying home, you and your kids will go through a honeymoon period. You will go out to lunch, you will go to the store in the middle of the day just because you can, you will take trips to the library or the museum. Then, one morning, you will wake up and realize that you are a little tired from all the running around you guys have been doing. This is when reality sets in. Being a SAHM is a marathon, not a sprint. You have to pace yourself.

At first, you will stay in with the kids for a few consecutive days, possibly doing crafts and games to keep yourselves occupied. Then a few more days later it will happen. You will be sitting with your kids, staring at each other, and you will all be wondering "OK, what do we do now?"

Then, something even more shocking will happen. You will feel bored. It may happen after a few weeks or it may take slightly longer, but boredom is a heavy, inescapable reality in the life of a SAHM. The job is exhausting, it is hard, but it is also monotonous, with days, weeks and years stretching out in front of you — a seemingly endless void depending on you to fill it. And you will. You will also occasionally catch a glimpse of yourself in the mirror and realize that you've barely combed your hair and you're still in your pajamas and its 2 o'clock in the afternoon.

Being an at home mom is not a cakewalk. There's an incredible amount of work involved with taking care of the house and your kids 24 hours a day, 7 days a week, 366 days a year. (Yes, I know there are only 365 days in a year, but it *feels* longer when you are a SAHM.) There will be days that the kids are sick of you. There will be days when you are sick of the kids. There will be days that you wonder what the heck you were thinking by staying home.

You need to realize two things about these feelings — they are completely normal and you are not a bad mom for having them. You are human and no human loves their job every single day. There are going to be good days and bad days and most, if not all, SAHM's go through the same exact things. Take heart, you are not in this boat alone.

5 Ways working outside the home is easier than being at home:
1. You have a starting and ending time. There is no time clock to punch at home and no second shift that comes in to relieve you.
2. You get mandatory breaks (even if you didn't take them, they were there). Breaks at home are called naps and during these breaks you get to fold laundry, pay bills and scrub toilets.
3. You can take vacation time. SAHM's define vacation time as buying toilet paper alone.
4. You get time away from your family. NASA should make shuttle tiles that stick as close as your family members.
5. You had sick time (C'mon, don't tell me that you never took the kids to the sitter and called in sick so you could be alone.)

I Know You Are, But What Am I?

Once you are home, you will have to deal with many different people's perceptions of what a typical SAHM is like. You will have to deal with your own preconceived notions as well. Your coworkers may be resentful, jealous or both. Strangers may look at you differently when they hear that "all you do" is stay home with your kids. People may actually look straight through you, as if you are not even there.

> *I remember shortly after I began staying at home, I had to take care of some insurance paperwork for my husband's business. I asked the agent a few questions about one of the policies, and he went on a ten minute diatribe that was on about a 6th grade level. I wanted to scream at him "I'm not an imbecile just because I stay at home — I have a degree for crying out loud!" It shocked me how differently I was treated.*

The point to remember throughout all this is: *why* you are home in the first place. You are there to raise your kids the way *you* see fit. *You* will be the one to take them to the park, *you* will be there to help out in their classroom and *you* will be there to take care of them when they are sick. All of the stress and drama, and yes, degradation that comes from making this transition are well worth the rewards.

The Bottom Line

Once you come to terms with how you got there, the next step is going to be figuring out how to run the house on a full time basis. You're going to need ways to deal with:

- Laundry - this is a never ending hamster wheel.
- Cooking - keep it simple, children are easy to please, and if yours are demanding Filet Mignon and Creme Brulee', that's your own darned fault.
- Keeping the house clean - dust is patient, it will wait. Large containers make quick clean-up easy.
- Keeping the kids clean — dirt is patient, it will wait. Seriously, unless your child doubles as a mole rat, he/she does not need a daily bath. A cursory once over with a couple baby wipes will hold them.
- Getting time to yourself — **MANDATORY**. Without it, *everyone* suffers. Happy moms = happy families.
- Having couple time with your husband — **MANDATORY**. Without it — *everyone* suffers. Happy parents = more kids, no wait, sorry...

It can be overwhelming, but if you accept the fact that there will be days where you wonder if you made the right decision *and* the fact that you will never get everything done, you will be well on your way to enjoying your time with your family.

Chapter 2:
The Myth of the Supermom

Remember the days back when you were working and you and your work friends who were moms would talk about the life of a stay at home mom and how perfect it must be? We're all eating those words now, aren't we? Would you like ketchup on yours?

Back then it seemed like at home moms had it all — they didn't have to get up for work, they didn't have to deal with pantyhose and they especially didn't have to deal with bosses. No worrying about rush hour commutes or picking up the kids from daycare on time. They also didn't have to deal with dreaded co-workers who spit when they talked or had never heard of deodorant.

It's the dreaded "Grass Is Always Greener" syndrome.

Ahhhh, look at what we have now. Our "bosses", who are around us 24/7, get to wake us up for work whenever they feel like it. In fact, sometimes we get stuck working the graveyard shift on top of our regular shift, which, oh by the way, never ends. Overtime is the norm. Vacation time doesn't exist. And sick days simply mean you throw up and keep going. Instead of rush hour commutes we have commutes to playgroups and music class. And as for the spitting co-worker? Well, if you have a baby or toddler you know all about being spit on.

The pressure to be a Supermom and get everything done that needs to be done is much worse as a SAHM. When we were working, we really thought SAHM's had all the time in the world to get their house clean, cook for the hubby and play educationally fun games with their kids. I mean, from the outside it certainly looked like they had all day, didn't it? On top of our own preconceived notions about at home moms, we have stereotypes like June Cleaver, Martha Stewart and Julia Childs mixed with the Super Nanny to guide us in our thinking. I hate to burst your bubble, but honey, June Cleaver is a myth and Martha wouldn't be Martha without a cadre of worker bees behind her success. As for Julia? Rest in peace, dear, you earned it.

Our reality is much different. How many times since you've been home have you looked at the clock, after having finally cleaned the kitchen from the morning rush, and realized that it was already time to make lunch?

Many new SAHM's think that because they are home, they will be able to craft the perfect life, complete with angelic kids, a clean and perfectly decorated house and piping hot meals on the table for the husband, daily. Then reality hits — the house is never pristine, the kids have a Lord of the Flies air about them, and a homemade meal is one that *made* it *home* from the drive-thru. New SAHM's tend to get thrown for the proverbial loop.

Forget trying to be a Supermom — it's way too stressful and who needs more stress? Besides super heroes tend to wear a lot of clingy Lycra and none of us needs *that*. We can't do it all and that's OK. Just because we don't leave the house for work doesn't mean that our life is going to be any easier. The earlier you can let go of these preconceived notions, the quicker you will be able to work on getting acclimated to the realities of your new life and get down to the business of enjoying your family.

The adjustment to SAHM-dom is not all doom and gloom, however, and just like when you worked outside the home, there will be days when everything clicks and you think to yourself "Hey, I really *can* do this." Remember and cling to those days. They will help get you through the ones that leave you wondering what on Earth you were thinking when you quit your job. Luckily, all the days — good and bad — balance out in the grand scheme of things and we can continue on as SAHM's without losing our minds (too much).

While you are transitioning, keep in mind that, as with any new endeavor from algebra to astrophysics, there is going to be a learning curve. No one is perfect right out of the box. Besides, perfection is boring and if you were perfect, you wouldn't have any good horror stories to tell when you got together with your other mom friends.

SAHM Myths vs. Realities

Myth #1 - Our houses are always clean.

Reality: If anything, they are messier because we are home more often. When we first begin staying home, we envision having the perfect, Architectural Digest house. Of course, reality hits about two days later when we realize that we can't even keep up with the kids, much less the messes, and that the only magazine cover we are suited for is Lesser Homes & Garbage.

Myth #2 - Our kids always eat healthy, balanced meals.

Reality: While you may do better in this area by now being home, you will still have days where they eat too much junk food. The problem is that while we now have more time to think about all the things we should and shouldn't be feeding them, we actually have less time to prepare and feed it to them. But as long as they don't know you by name in the McDonald's drive-thru, and you throw in some foods that were actually grown on a tree and not in a can or laboratory, it will all balance out.

Myth #3 - Our laundry is always clean, pressed and neatly put away.
Reality: Based on the fact that laundry seems to grow exponentially once you begin staying home, you will need to quickly come to terms with the fact that you will never be fully caught up with it. Ever. Sure, you will have some weeks where you feel you have dominion over the never ending piles, but on the whole, most weeks your laundry won't even make it to a dresser or hanger before it is in a dirty pile again.

Myth #4 - We cook three course meals for our family on a nightly basis - no more takeout!
Reality: Ha! There are several reasons this may not happen. One — Have you tried cooking gourmet meals with little kids underfoot? Most of us never did it when we were young, single and romancing full speed ahead, so why should we think we will pull off some culinary miracle now that we have miniature sous chefs banging on all the pots and pans? Two — When you are home it is easier to lose track of time. You may *want* to cook lamb chops with a creamy asparagus sauce, but when you think its 3 pm and look at the clock only to discover it's really 5:30 pm, it isn't likely to happen. Three — What if you can't even cook? Unfortunately Betty Crocker is on a box, not in our genes. There is no magic switch that gets flipped when you turn into a SAHM. If you can't cook, you will need to learn some basic strategies, like boiling

water and using the microwave oven, to make cooking a little easier on you.

Myth #5 - Our kids should always behave properly because we are home with them all the time.

Reality: If only. Just because we are with the kids all the time doesn't mean that they aren't going to misbehave. Kids will be kids, whether they are with Mom, Dad, grandparents, or even Santa Claus (you've seen how those kids act while waiting in line). The benefit here is that instead of fighting with the kids at daycare, they can now fight with you or their siblings. Don't expect miracles. You can be comforted by the fact that regardless of how they act, you are the one shaping their behavior. Depending on the day, this is a fact that may or may not make you feel better.

The Bottom Line

The bottom line is this — the myth of the Supermom is just that, a myth. You are a mother, not a Mother Teresa, and will not be performing miracles just by virtue of your new position. (Don't worry though. God saves a special halo for SAHM's.) Don't put too much pressure on yourself. Being a homemaker and raising kids full-time is tough enough without attempting to be Martha Stewart's apprentice and the Queen of the PTA too. Just take each day as it comes and be happy with the job you are doing. Find at least one thing each day that could not have happened if you weren't *there* — even if it is something as silly as a finger painting or a tickle fight — *your presence* made it happen. In the overall scheme of things it won't matter if your house was cleaner or messier than the Suzy Homemaker down the street. It *will* matter that you had fun with your kids.

Chapter 3:
Husbands Just Don't Understand

The first time I mentioned staying home with our daughter instead of working full time, my husband laughed. 'If you do,' he said, 'you'd better have the house immaculate all the time — no dust on the picture frames, floors always swept.' Talk about pressure.

- Pam K., Ohio

Husbands deserve, nay require, special attention. When you decide to stay home, he's probably going to have mixed feelings. His idea of a SAHM will probably be much different than what you have in mind. Think about it this way — the only knowledge he probably has of what a SAHM does may only go so far as what he has seen on TV. You know the June Cleaver-Carol Brady syndrome? If his mother was a SAHM, had white carpet with plastic over the furniture *and* she was president of the PTA, watch out — you have a long road ahead of you.

Having a stay at home wife can actually be threatening for a guy. It forces him to mentally switch roles and become the SOLE breadwinner, and while there is a certain amount of machismo derived from this, it is also a point that may actually lead him to experience random and intense flashes of panic. It's also going to be a bit confusing for him. Poor man, he's used to having a hard working wife who was easy to view as an equal, but who now wants to go and erase her salary completely so she can, in his eyes anyway, become some 1950's stereotype.

Be patient. As much as you are realizing what's actually

involved in the new role, he will be too. But since he is not home with you, it will take longer for him to fully grasp what you are now doing all day long and the important role you are now playing in your family's dynamic. Again, be patient. Initially, chances are he just won't get it. I'm not talking about that 'it,' but if has a difficult time transitioning, he may not get *that* it either. He's not going to have any idea what to expect, how he should react or how you will react. Be gentle with him...to a point. While he's not going to understand how you feel after being home with the kids all day, and he probably won't understand why when he gets home after 5, dinner isn't on the table and you are still in your pajamas, and he's definitely not going to understand why the house looks like a tornado tore through it, his lack of comprehension should not be allowed to acquit bad behavior on his part.

It's going to be up to you to help him understand how things work when you are at home. And even though you have probably already done it once, he's going to have to be retrained. You are there to raise the kids, not to be Mrs. Brady. In fact, Carol had Alice to do all the heavy lifting for her. He needs to understand that you two are still a team, with the same ultimate goal of raising your children the way you both want them raised. Inform him that if his goal is to have a super clean house, he can hit the ground running when he comes in the door at night or hire a housekeeper to help you *both* out, preferably one named Alice.

Communication is the key

The only true way to help your husband understand what you are going through is to communicate. It's going to be crucial that you talk with him about how you are feeling *and that he listens.* After all, you are the one who is redefining your identity and this is not an easy transition. Open lines of communication will bypass any resentment and ensure you both feel supported and are still a team.

Sure, he may not understand why you are crying about missing work when a few months ago you were crying about missing the kids. And he might not understand why it is so vital that you have time for yourself or why you might actually want to get out of the house without the kids every once in a while. That's only because he hasn't done what you are doing. Any man, left alone for one solid week as a SAHD, would never question any of the above. In fact, SAHD Boot Camp ought to be a mandatory rite of passage.

You simply have to let him know what your needs are. If you need to get some "me" time every day for 30 minutes, tell him, and then take it. If you want to get together with your girlfriends once a month, tell him and then do it. He will quickly see the benefits both he and the family unit reaps in allowing you to be more than a mommy. Just remember, he might be the best husband in the world, but he is still a guy and he is going to need some help figuring out the new roadmap for this situation.

Another idea that may work for you is this — men, like many other primal animals, work well with a reward system. Reward them for their good behavior and there is a very good chance that it will be repeated. If positive reinforcement can work with kids, then it can definitely work with husbands. Substitute your own reward, but pick one that will show your hubby, leaving no doubt in his mind, that whatever he did should be repeated, and often. The first and most obvious reward that comes to mind is sex. Now, I am not saying that you should withhold sex just to get your way — that is juvenile and manipulative — regardless of how effective it is. However, depending on how desperate you are to get your needs met, you may have to pull out the heavy artillery. But hey, if your needs are met *and* his needs are met, you ultimately will both be happy campers.

How Can I Feel Sexy In a Ketchup Stained Shirt?

One of the things you will quickly learn about being a SAHM is that it can sometimes be difficult to shift gears from Mommy to Hot Mama. When it's 9 p.m. and your husband is giving you *that* look, it can be a challenge to look at your husband with little more than indifference. After a day of being pulled on, screamed at, wiped on and stressed out, intimacy is probably the furthest thing from your mind. And while your hubby should definitely cut you some emotional slack, he also needs to up the ante on romance. It's amazing what a few candles, a back rub and some whispered sweet nothings can do to help you switch gears from functional to fun. And for your part, while you should never feel forced to do something you truly are not up for, if you let yourself relax and wrap your mind around feeling sexy and wanted, you'll end the evening wondering why you two don't do this more often.

One perk to being a SAHM? You don't have to worry about getting up for work or commuting in rush hour traffic, which is stress relieving enough to increase the romance factor significantly.

Ways to Make Intimacy Easier Once You Are a SAHM

You may discover that despite being constantly exhausted by the kids, keeping the romance alive is something that may actually get easier when you begin staying at home. Subtracting worrying about bosses, coworkers, deadlines and other work related junk frees up a lot of time to think about other things. And even if money is tight, intimacy, and namely sex, is still free and reaps better dividends than any corporate merger. Your romantic relationship with your husband grows stronger and though it may sound crazy, after a late night with the hubby, getting up with the kids is WAY easier than getting up to go face a job. SAHM could stand for Sexy At Home Mom, you know.

Here's a few ways to make that S in SAHM stand for Sexy:

Schedule a regular date night with your husband.

Yes, the whole idea of Date Night is terribly cliché, but after being around the kids all day, it will be even more imperative for you and your husband to reconnect. It's important to remember why you fell in love in the first place. Even if you just do something low cost, like a bottle of wine after the kids are tucked in, or free, like swapping backrubs while you reminisce about your dating days, couple time is crucial time. It strengthens your relationship, which in turn strengthens the family.

Make sure you get some time to yourself each night to help you transition from Mom to Wife.

When you were working, you had your commute to decompress and prepare for your evening time with the family. With that time now gone, you need to make sure you find it other ways. When the kids go to bed, ask your husband to wait a few minutes to make his move and take those extra minutes for yourself, even if it's only 15 minutes to read a book. This is especially helpful if you have clingy kids. When you have kids clinging to you all day, then your husband wants to cling to you, it can lead to frustration instead of friskiness. Explain to your husband you need a few minutes alone so you don't feel like a piece of mommy cling wrap, then spend those minutes doing some deep breathing, relaxing and reconnecting with your sexy side.

Surprise your husband every now and then.

If he is used to seeing you in t-shirts and sweats every day, mix it up a bit. Throw on a v-neck sweater and some perfume. If you feel more desirable wearing make up, get up early enough to put some on before he leaves in the morning or put it on before he gets home at night. Sexy is a state of mind and it is amazing what little effort it takes to get you there. While you don't have to put on a show for him nightly, breaking out of the norm can make things more interesting for both of you.

Don't just talk about the kids and the house.

After a tough day at work, your hubby might not want a run down about the fights or the washing machine that's on the fritz. When you were working, your conversations were probably more balanced between work and family issues. Make more of an effort to keep in touch with things going on in the real world. Watch the evening news once in a while, stop by CNN.com for a few minutes each day, or scan the headlines of the newspaper during naptime. Stay informed, stay opinionated and be able to hold your own in an adult conversation. Being able to talk about something other than the kids will increase your confidence and make it easier to get in the mood, more than if you just yammer on about the latest kid and house drama. Bottom line: Keep him up to date about day to day goings on, but unless it's earth shattering (someone took their first steps, lost a tooth, won a soccer game) or expensive (time for a new washer/dryer/car), give him the Cliff Notes version and then talk about the world and each other.

Husbands and the House — You Are Not A Maid

Once you begin staying home and you get a feel for what you can and cannot accomplish during the day, you need to sit down and talk with him about it. It is his house too and once he understands that you are *both* still working, he needs to find ways he can help out around the house when he is home. One trap you don't want to fall into is allowing him to think you should do everything around the house just because he leaves for work every day and you don't. Lay it out that during the day *your* job is to raise your kids and what you are doing for the family cannot be measured in money. In fact, he doesn't make enough money to actually pay for the services you are providing and the time you are clocking.

Some husbands have a hard time understanding this. If your husband is one of these, stick to your guns. People, even husbands, will treat you the way you allow yourself to be treated. You need to stress the importance of him helping out around the house. That it will set a good example for the kids, and at the very least, he will have a much happier wife. If this is a continual sticking point despite your attempts to communicate, you may have to take drastic measures and, like so many a SAHM's has done before you, go on a temporary strike. More than a few men have been changed forever when their wives stopped doing their laundry, cooking and cleaning up after them. Basic human nature dictates that you cannot truly appreciate something until you no longer have it. Even guys have their breaking point; if you've been pushed to yours, the key is to find his.

Resentment, Jealousy and Other Reasons to Be Mad At Your Husband

Resentment & Jealousy

When I first began staying home, I was warned by one of my SAHM friends. "Just wait until you turn on your own husband. That's when you know you are a true SAHM."

My first thought was that she was a little loopy from being cooped up in the house too long. Then it happened to me. Nothing earth shaking or apocalyptic — it was just a day like any other day before it — however, my reaction to the new "normal" of my life was cataclysmic.

My unsuspecting husband got up, just like he does each day, and went to work, just like he does every day.

As I watched him leave, something snapped. The rope that had safely held my psyche to its dock, shredded and I felt my sanity slip from its moorings into a sea of resentment. Adrift in these new emotions, I caught myself thinking "Look at him. Sure, I don't have to get up and leave every morning, but he gets to go away and just be himself every day."

I spent that day floundering in the deep blues of the SAHM ocean.

Another indicator that you may be in need of a mental tow rope is when your husband crosses the threshold of your home and you immediately thrust the kids at him while screaming, "I can't take it anymore and I need a few moments to myself!" over your shoulder as you go lock yourself in the bathroom.

Resentment is at the heart of this storm and if you honestly identify it, you have a much better shot at surviving it. Having turned your entire world inside out and upside down for what often times seems like little appreciation and no validation, it is easy to slip on those emerald colored glasses — you know, the ones that make the grass look greener on the other side of the fence?

Money issues can also highlight this tension. When you go from making the money to feeling like you're always asking for it, your ego takes another blow, especially if money is tight. You need to work this one out early in the game and the earlier the better. At no point should you feel or be viewed as subservient or that you have to ask for permission simply because you are no longer bringing in a paycheck. Again, your husband does not make enough money to pay all the people you are, including a cook, caterer, taxi driver, child care provider, personal shopper, nurse, maid, butler, nanny, seamstress, secretary, laundress, dry cleaner, interior decorator, teacher, tutor, hotelier, hostess, handywoman, landscaper, poolboy, and on and on. Since he may be harboring his own resentment at you being home while he is out sacrificing for the family, communication is again the key. You have to talk and you have to stay equal players on the same team. If either of you does not feel like you are being listened to, resentment will take you straight to the bottom of the relationship ocean. But if you commit to being one another's safe place, lighthouse, and life preserver — calm winds and smooth sailing will prevail.

Guys' Night Out

Guys' night out is probably one of the most hated nights as a mom. They may be an irritant when you work outside the home, but they become a full blown allergy when you are a stay at home mom. He is gone *all day* for work and then he gets to rush home so he can *leave again* and go be with his *guy friends?* I don't think so! I mean, when the closest thing you have had to adult interaction in months is Big Bird on Sesame Street, how is that fair?

Surprisingly, "fair" depends on you. Do you make sure to have activities planned just for you that don't involve your kids or your husband or running errands? Do you maintain your female friendships? If not, then while you will probably be pretty mad as your husband goes off for a guy's night out, you truly only have yourself to blame. I said this in the beginning — no matter how well intentioned your husband is, even he is not always going to give you what you need. You need to stand up and take it, knowing that everyone will benefit.

As for his nights out? I'm going to fill you in on why you should let him go and see him off with a smile.

First of all, guys are wired differently than women. I realize that's not a secret or anything, but guys gain something from being around other men. They derive comfort from being with people who don't care if, or where, they scratch and who don't judge them when they act obnoxious or do all the things that generally drive their wives nuts. Just as it is good for you to bond with your girls, it's good for them to go be with their kind, especially if you run the house. While with the guys, they can brag and act like the ruler of their domain because their wives aren't around to hear it. (And yes, the other guys know it's all total crap because they live the exact same lives in their homes, but they allow one another to pretend anyway.)

Secondly, if you are truly mad about it, you need to examine how much of your anger is your responsibility and how much is actually, legitimately his fault. Is it because he spends too much money when he goes out? Talk to him about it. Explain that it simply isn't in your budget *for either of you* to spend that much when out with friends. It's hard for him to protest if you both have the same rules to play by. Are you mad because you don't get to go out too? If that is the case, get over it, make some phone calls and gets some dates out with your friends written *in ink* on your calendar. You are entitled to be your own person just like he is. Make sure he recognizes this fact. When he sees how much happier you are when you do get to go off and do your own thing, he will most likely be very supportive and begin insuring you getting the time you need.

We may be more sophisticated than our Neanderthal husbands, with our ability to think with both sides of our brains at one time and coordinate our shoes with our purses, but we can still benefit from a pressure releasing night out with the girls where we can act catty, gossipy and even petty.

Not that we women are like that, but you get my point.

The Bottom Line

Husbands are great — they can be our biggest cheerleaders, strongest support systems and best friends. Just remember, that as your decision to stay home was a joint one, so is the transition that comes with it. You will both be thrown off balance initially. Keep your expectations of one another realistic, communicate like you've never communicated before, state very plainly what your needs are, give one another the freedom to maintain outside interests and friends, and always carve out time to maintain your love relationship. As long as you both equally *give* as much as you *take*, you can both weather the transition and become all the stronger for it. You are in this together. Period. And once your lives adjust to the new definition of "normal", you will find that there is more *quality* time to be a couple and that your bond is deeper than ever before.

SECTION 2
Um, Okay. Now What?

Chapter 4:
Now That I'm Home, What on Earth Do I Do?

Chapter 5:
SAHM Does Not Stand For Stuck At Home Mom

Chapter 6:
Stuck In the Land of the Little People

Chapter 4:
Now That I'm Home, What On Earth Do I Do?

It was a couple weeks after I began staying home that I had my first inkling that things were going to be very different than I had envisioned. Having been to the mall, the libraries, the bookstores and the park, exhausting every type of recreational venue I could think of, I was at home with my son and we both just kind of sat there looking at each other. It was one thing to be home on the weekends, but this being home and keeping him entertained on a daily basis was more challenging than I ever thought it would be.

While enough to make even the staunchest of teetotalers' tip one, the realization that you are going to be solely responsible for the entertainment of your kids is actually a very sobering thought. Factor in trying to keep up with the dust bunnies and the cobwebs and it can be downright frightening at first. Suddenly you've gone from being a thoughtful, contributing member of the adult world to being the Julie McCoy of your very own Love Boat, only in addition to planning all activities on the Ledo Deck, you have to clean the entire ship. Oh, and your boat never seems to dock in Puerto Vallarta. It simply sails in one big, monotonous circle.

So what's a new SAHM to do to keep her children amused and intellectually stimulated every day? First of all — don't panic.

Before you call your old boss and beg to have your job back, keep this in mind — there *will* be days when you are bored, days when your kids are bored and days when you are both bored to tears. As long as you can accept this fact and understand that the mind numbingly boring days, when time actually seems to move backwards, are the *exception*, **not the rule**, you and your kids will survive. Here are some tips for those days when you feel like jumping overboard...

Around the House

Don't feel like you have to buy a warehouse full of toys to keep the kids entertained. The old adage about kids liking the box something comes in better than the actual toy is absolutely true. This is because children are a symbol of creativity and imagination. Take advantage of this. The best toys are often the things you already have. Cardboard boxes, pots and pans, old catalogs, and plastic bowls and spoons are particular favorites in my house. These improvised "toys" will help to expand your child's imagination better than any electronic talking gizmo. One day my son actually made his own laptop computer using a box, some tin foil, and a toy piano. He even incorporated one of his baby sister's toys to use as a mouse. This innovative (a.k.a. cheap) toy kept him busy and entertained for three solid days.

Old Box: $0.00

Tin Foil: $0.25

Child Occupied So Mom Can Clean Toilets And Mop Floors: PRICELESS

Kids and the Boob Tube

Yes, I'm going to get into the whole TV debate thing even though you've surely been bombarded with the "perils of TV watching" since your pregnancy test came back positive. But as a former teacher, I feel I have to put in my two cents. And those two cents will buy you four syllables: Mod-er-a-tion. Yes, moderation, that same watchword used to regulate our intake of fast food, alcohol and candy. (Although when it comes to chocolate, is there really such a thing as *too* much? Don't answer, I have PMS — it was a rhetorical question.)

In terms of moderation and content, I am all for letting your kids watch a few cartoons. We all did it while growing up and don't seem to be scarred for life by marathon viewings of Bugs Buggy and Schoolhouse Rock. My suggestion though is that you institute some type of time limit. My kids get to watch one hour in the morning and are allowed to choose a movie before they go to bed. We fill those hours in between with reading, playtime and imagination. But that's not to say there aren't occasional exceptions. While constantly using the television as babysitter is simply a bad habit to fall into, never feel like a rotten parent if you happen to allow them an extra Dora or Blue's Clues episode or pop in a short video so you can complete an important project, finish up the dishes or even go to the bathroom by yourself.

Coloring & Crafts

One of the easiest and cheapest ways to keep kids entertained is with coloring and craft projects. Even if you have lived most of your life 'craft-ually challenged' you will be amazed at your ability to learn and also dream up original, fun activities for your kids. It's called survival and we human beings are good at it. To make your job easier and keep your creative juices flowing, try to keep some basic supplies on hand and make use of your computer to help you when your juices run dry like Aunt Mildred's Thanksgiving turkey. With Google at your fingertips, you can surf craft projects for all age levels and abilities, print out coloring sheets and even find websites where your child can color online.

Here are some basic art supplies to keep on hand:
• Crayons
• Chalk
• Watercolor Paints
• Markers (There is a special place reserved in heaven for the person who created the Washable versions!)
• Construction Paper
• Old Scrap Paper - Recycled computer paper works great.
• Pipe Cleaners
• Glue/Glue Sticks
• Safety Scissors
• Glitter - It's completely messy, which means kids love it even more. (Quick clean-up tip: Keep a lint roller on hand. A couple easy swipes and VOILA! - glitter-free surfaces.)
• Foam Pieces - These are precut shapes in a nice squishy foam. Great for any project and you can find them in both regular and with self adhesive on the backs.
• Old Catalogs - These are great for scavenger hunts and cutting practice.

Coloring has to be the one of the defining activities of childhood. Nowadays the coloring resources are mind-boggling. Besides traditional coloring books, there are online coloring sites for virtually everything your child might like. Here is a basic list of some of the more commercial sites. If you don't see whatever is "it" at your house, just type it into a search engine like Google or Yahoo. The official site is usually closest to the top.

- Nick Jr. (www.nickjr.com) includes Blue's Clues and Dora the Explorer.
- Playhouse Disney on Disney Online (www.playhousedisney.com) has Rolie Polie Olie and Stanley.
- PBS Kids (www.pbskids.com) includes Clifford, Arthur and Dragon Tales among many, many others.
- Sesame Street (www.sesameworkshop.com) has all of your favorite Sesame Street characters, including Elmo.

The nice thing about these sites is that they have great parent areas and newsletters you can subscribe to (as long as you love getting email). The worst part about these sites is that they also sell merchandise, so be careful that you don't accidentally hit one of *those* links while your little one is watching, otherwise you may end up with a kid whining for the latest and greatest toy from their favorite character.

If you are looking for something less commercial, there are plenty of generic coloring sheet sites on the internet. One of the biggest is Coloring.ws (www.coloring.ws). If your child wants to color a picture of something obscure, say a seashell, racecar or Tyrannosaurus Rex, check here first. One thing to watch out for when you are scanning the net for craft websites is that some of the "coloring" websites are just advertisements for other products, so you may have to wade through some garbage to finally strike gold.

Having a basic supply of arts and crafts items available at all times can be a lifesaver when you have a bored kid on your hands. How do you cheer up a "Whine-asaurus?" The key is to throw them off their usual routine. Washable finger paints are great, messy fun. Not only can the kids color on paper, but they can color on themselves as well. If they are particularly messy while painting, stick them in the bathtub. This way they can paint all they want — the tub, the walls, each other, you — and clean up is as easy as turning on the water. Another way to cheer up a cranky kid is to let them color with something other than crayons. One mom I know swears by cheap chalk. It is a little messier than crayons, but worth it when you see the results. Grab some colored construction paper and let them go to town. If weather permits, set your little Picassos loose on the sidewalk or a back patio. They will stay occupied for hours, think they are getting away with something and the mess is self cleaning — just wait for the next rain. Plus, if they are allowed to go crazy on the driveways, you never know, maybe they won't be tempted to color on the walls.

There are a plethora of ingenious websites packed with seemingly infinite ideas for fun and easy crafts. The benefits of going online for craft information are 1) You don't have to be creative — simply bask in the glow of someone else's imagination, and 2) Many of the sites have pictures of the finished products so you have an idea of what you are striving towards. My favorite site is DLTK's Printable Crafts for Kids (www.dltk-kids.com). This site has crafts for everything imaginable, including holidays, animals, cartoon characters, numbers and letters, and of course, old standbys like princesses and dump trucks. Another good site to try is Enchanted Learning (www.enchantedlearning.com). They are more educationally based than DLTK's, so you'll see a lot of educational games, fairy tale activities and even a printable, colorable picture dictionary. For more resources than you could ever fully exhaust, check the resources section at the end of the book.

Let's Get Physical

One of the most difficult things about being home with your kids is trying to keep them active enough to actually burn off energy, and we all know young children have barrels full. If the world's scientists could figure out how to harness the power cells of a preschooler, we would never have to drill for oil again. Because my kids are *very* active, I have become an expert at inventing new ways to help them burn off energy productively. The preferred activity rotates from week to week, but here are some of their favorites:

Obstacle Courses

> Once you've been home for a while, you'll learn that you can make an obstacle course out of just about anything. (This is where letting go of those illusions of the perfectly cleaned, straightened house come into play.) All you need to do is make sure there is jumping, crawling, scooting or running involved. We have used pillows (both from the couch and from the bed), blocks, cars

and even bowls. Set up trails around furniture, through hallways and even up the stairs if you have them and your little one can navigate them safely.

Dancing

One of the most entertaining things to do as a parent is watch your children dance. My kids never cease to amaze me with the moves they come up with. I am not a big fan of traditional children's music and luckily my kids aren't either, so I try to find regular music without any objectionable material. Expose your kids to different types of music from reggae to classical to oldies and then let them gravitate towards their favorite. Right now my son is favoring Top 40 and boy bands (much to my husband's dismay). For generally safe, non-offensive music, check out the soundtracks to your kids' favorite movies.

Playing Outside

I'm going to sound old and curmudgeonly on this one, but one of the things I have noticed about kids growing up these days is that they are so busy playing Game Boy and watching TV that they don't know how to play outside anymore. Sound crazy? It's not. When was the last time you saw a bunch of kids playing Kick the Can or Hide -n- Seek? Some of my best childhood memories are of playing outside with my friends. As parents of younger kids we can help change this trend.

Take your kids for a walk to the park or go outside and kick a ball around. Go on a nature scavenger hunt and look for leaves or rocks for a collection. Play tag. You can even just sit outside and look at the clouds. Whatever you do, just be sure everyone goes potty first and that you pack water and a snack. In fact, the mere act of packing up some crackers and water bottles turns even a simple walk around the block into an adventure hike. Besides, there is nothing more frustrating than getting half way to the park and hearing "Mom, I'm hungry!" or even worse "Mommy, I have to go potty!"

Take It Down a Notch

Everyone needs downtime — even children. And teaching yours that quiet time is OK time is very important. So slow down the pace a bit each day, there are plenty of ways to keep the kids calm and entertained. Try some of these:

Read A Book

Sure, this is another one of those parenting tips that has been hammered into our heads since we became parents, but again, as a former teacher, I cannot stress enough how important this is. It *does* make a difference. The best way to learn about a language is to be immersed in it. Reading to a child helps them begin to understand how language works. Take regular walks through your library's children's section and let your child pick out their own books. In fact, allow your child to get their very own library card so they feel a sense of ownership over reading. Besides having a wide variety of books from which to choose, they will feel more involved in the process, which in turn makes them more likely to enjoy it. Of course, if they pick out one that you aren't happy with or isn't acceptable, you can always sneak it back while you are checking out.

As a variation to this theme, let them try to "read" the book to you. Have them tell you a story based on the pictures. You can also encourage them to look through magazines. If they are older, have them look for words they recognize. Sometimes a little novelty is all it takes to keep kids entertained. Just make sure you screen the magazine first — Little Suzy probably won't need to look through last month's Cosmo with the article "25 Secrets to Better Sex."

Anything With Water

If it is warm enough outside and you have a back yard, why not let them play with the garden hose? They can water the grass or flowers or even play firefighter. Another fantastic water works idea is to let them wash your car. A couple squirts of dish soap or baby shampoo in a bucket, a few colorful sponges and soon your vehicle is streaky clean — yes, *streaky*, not squeaky. Get over it. The memories you will make are well worth the trade off of having a slightly less than perfect wash job. For smaller children, let them pull up a chair to the sink and practice pouring water into different containers. This also works well in the bathtub.

For bigger hands, try giving your kids a spray bottle full of water. They can spray it on the sidewalk, the kitchen sink, even straight into the air as long as you don't mind a little mist on the carpet. It'll dry quickly and will temporarily calm even the feistiest of kids.

Play Doh

Play Doh has to be one of the greatest inventions of all time. And, in what I'm convinced is one of the biggest ironies in parenting, it is also one of the activities we Moms and Dads despise the most. It's like someone said "Here, you can have this great toy that will diffuse virtually any stressful situation, but clean up after its use will be a nightmare."

If one of the kids is having a particularly cranky day or you simply need a little breathing room, pull out the Play Doh and Voila! — entertainment for hours! To make it even more interesting and fun, provide them with cookie cutters, plastic utensils and a plastic cup to use as a rolling pin. By using this secret weapon, you may actually buy yourself enough time to fold a load of laundry right out of the dryer or even cook dinner.

Back to the irony: this miracle toy does come with a price in that no child has ever been able to keep their Play Doh on the table, tarp or sheet put underneath them. It will be EVERYWHERE. Tip: If it gets in the carpet, LET IT DRY. You will have much better luck scraping it out and vacuuming it up. If it is still damp, you can try to use some fresh Play Doh to roll up the bigger fallen pieces. And if it is ground into your carpet (or your kid's hair), either get used to the new technicolor scheme or grab a pair of scissors. Little Joey needed a haircut anyway, right?

The Bottom Line

Now that you have a list of ideas for getting your kids active and keeping them entertained around the house, you need to always keep the most important point in the front of your mind: **Have fun.** Remember *why* you wanted to stay home with them in the first place. They won't know the difference if you go to one class versus another; nor will they care if you do a craft with them that comes out a little "different looking" (trust me, I speak from experience). All they will care about is that they are getting to spend time with their favorite person on the face of the planet. Remember, while you are stressing about "planning" something for them to do, they are simply excited that you are home with them.

Chapter 5:

Be a Stay At Home Mom, Not a *Stuck* At Home Mom

Well, now you've gone and done it. Remember all that time you spent secretly (or not so secretly) making fun of SAHM's when you were playing hooky from work? You know, watching them as they drank their lattes while their kids accosted other kids at the mall, seeing them drive by in their semi-sized SUV's on the way to the gym (how do they manage to do THAT?), or hearing about their new decorating project while in line at the craft store. Admit it, you looked down your far superior nose, scoffing at their carts full of craft sticks and felt squares.

And now, you big hypocrite, YOU ARE ONE OF THEM!

Ok, well, you probably aren't fully one of them — yet.

Isn't it amusing that as soon as we begin staying home with our kids, we immediately start looking for activities to put them into? "Yes my darling child, I am staying home to be with you. Now let's see what classes the Parks & Recreation department has that you can join!" Sure, it's possible we do this because we are genuinely happy to be able to allow them to participate in things that were not possible when they were confined to daycare, but if we're honest, we seek these extracurricular activities out to take some of the entertaining pressure off ourselves. And there are a ton of activity choices out there for every budget and interest.

Even with all the options available, one of the things new SAHM's need to do is keep their child's schedule reasonable. While it's fun to go to Gymboree and swim classes, *too much* makes for a cranky kid. Too many activities means endless transport time, getting the kids in and out of the car, and having lunch on the go. More importantly, oftentimes naps are missed and all moms know that a missed nap is an open invitation for disaster. Don't avoid classes altogether, they are fun and help your child socialize, just pace yourself and don't overload your day on a regular basis. Strive for balance. If you have one really busy day, follow it up with two or three slower paced ones.

On the flip side of this issue, don't stay confined to the house all the time either. As important as peer time is for your child, it is equally as imperative that you get some type of adult interaction, even if it is just with the lady in the grocery store check out line. This kind of interaction reaffirms that you are still capable of having an adult conversation between the hours of 7am and 5pm.

It's A Jungle Out There

So, you know to avoid over-scheduling your child, but what *is* out there for them to do? Many new SAHM's are on some type of budget, so it is important to keep that in mind when looking. There are many places where you can find fun, enriching, low to no cost activities to do with your kids. The top places to look are:

1. The Public Library
2. Community Parenting Programs
3. Free Parenting Magazines
4. Your Local Mall
5. Your Housing Community
6. Extra-Curricular Activities

The Public Library

Even if you haven't set foot in a library since you were in high school or college, once you have a child you should definitely become familiar with the one in your community. The most obvious reason is for the free books. Even babies enjoy being read to, it is quality bonding time and checking books out from the library ensures that you have a no-cost variety to choose from. Once your child is a little older, usually around the one year mark, you can begin going to story time. Library story time can be a fun, educational activity to share with your child, not to mention a fantastic way for you to meet other parents.

Story time usually includes the reading of two or three books, plus songs, felt board stories, and a special treat at the end, usually stickers or a coloring sheet. Again, the best things about these types of programs is that they are free *and* they keep kids' attention for 30-40 minutes.

Libraries, however, are not the only places to catch a story time. Many of the major bookstores sponsor at least one special story time per month. One of the major ones in my area does it every Tuesday and Saturday, and theirs includes crafts and stickers, as well as the stories. Check with the book stores in your area; if they don't currently have one, ask them to consider adding one. What bookstore wouldn't want a dozen kids screaming at their parents to buy their books on a regular basis?

Community Programs

Many communities are making more of an effort to offer parenting resources and family friendly activities. With recent research highlighting the importance of strong families for children's development, communities are jumping on the bandwagon to help out. There are typically two types of programs communities offer: city art and recreation classes and community youth classes.

City art and recreation classes are usually offered through the local city parks and recreation department. Many parks and rec departments offer both physical recreation classes and art classes. They are a reasonably priced way to introduce your child to many different types of activities, which helps them define what their interests are. Classes may include such things as pottery, dance, basic arts and crafts, music, mom and tot classes and even preschool sports classes. The instructors are usually local college students, teachers, or moms with school age kids, so instruction quality is reliable.

Other types of community programs are becoming popular. The United Way offers youth programs in cities across the country. The benefit of these is that they strive to teach the importance of a strong family unit and the importance of education. One program in my community, called "Family Fun Van," is for kids ages 0-5. It is offered 4 times a week at sites throughout the city. The program includes story time, a physical activity (like games or parachute time), free play time with a variety of toys, craft time, and snack time. The best part? It's free *and* each family receives a free book! My kids received books like Sandra Boynton's *Pajama Time* and books from the Clifford the Big Red Dog series.

Each week of the program has a theme with all activities tailored to it. The most popular theme of the year is usually firefighter week. Not only do the kids receive fire hats and stickers, but they also get a visit from the local fire station. Not surprisingly, this week always has the best turnout. I'm not sure who is more excited to see the firefighters though — the kids or the moms.

Local Parenting Magazines

You may not be aware of your local parenting magazine, but chances are you have passed by it dozens of times. They are usually on your way out of the grocery store or library and sadly, are often overlooked. I say *sadly* because they contain a wealth of information. Many of these free magazines are monthly and follow specific themes, such as Mother's Day and Choosing A Summer Camp. They have articles on parenting, but also include sections with local resources for kids as well as a calendar of events, listing any that are kid friendly, including special seasonal events, theater performances and kid's day at the museum. I know many moms who scan the calendar and plan events for each week of the month.

The Local Mall

I realize that many of us moms do not need any excuses…I mean reasons, to go to the mall, however, for those who do, there are quite a few malls which sponsor special activities for young children. (Rest assured, I do not counting riding up and down the escalator 25 times an activity.) Barring predictable holiday events, there are two items you should look for: a kids' club and a play place.

In an attempt to lure desperate parents to the mall on a regular basis, many malls offer some type of kids' club. These clubs typically have some generic mascot (who is usually worse than Barney and the Teletubbies combined) and a host who attempts to keep 100 screaming toddlers and preschoolers under control while singing extremely irritating songs at a piercing octave. They even have weekly themes. Despite the irritation factors, they usually strive for some level of combined fun and "education" in their programs. They sing songs and get the kids involved in various "helper" activities, like leading the songs and passing out supplies. They also give out stickers and activity sheets along with coupons to the local stores. Now your kids will ask to go to the mall, and you can tell your husband that you simply *must* take them because not only is it all in the name of fun for the kids, but it is completely FREE. And, oh yeah, did I show you my new shoes and matching purse, dear?

The other fun reason to take the kids to the mall (like we need another reason) is the Play Place. This is the area in the mall with giant shoes, apples, dollhouses and other oversized apparatus for kids to play on. The climbing pieces are made of a durable plastic material and the floor is a thick, padded cushion that gives when kids inevitably fall. My children absolutely love playing here. It is completely enclosed, so there is only one way in and out. There are paths for the kids to follow that resemble a giant game board, and activities to complete based upon the square on which they land. If you aren't sure whether your mall has one of these, just walk to the middle of the facility and stand quietly for a minute. If you hear what sounds like a herd of screaming elephants, then your mall has a Play Place. Simply follow the shrieking, or if that doesn't work, watch for the mom who is dragging a screaming child and walk to wherever they came from.

Your Housing Community

Many housing developments, in an effort to bring together families and neighbors, are offering various activities and classes for their residents. If you live in one of those huge master planned communities, chances are you have a clubhouse with some sort of activity program. If so, ask to speak to the programming director about the types of activities they offer or touch base with your Home Owner's Association.

If you live in a community that doesn't have any neighborhood programs, ask about starting one. If there is a resident willing to do the footwork, many places will gladly offer up the space in return. If you have a special talent such as dance or piano, offer to teach a class for kids. It will give you a way to meet other children, network with moms in your neighborhood and may even earn you a little spending money.

Extracurricular Activities

Extracurricular activities are the defining feature of being a SAHM. According to the myth, we load up our minivans on a daily basis to forge into the world of sports or music or drama. We unrelentingly cheer on our precious offspring, no matter their skill level. Some of us even get involved in the activity, whether or not we were asked to. The myth *is*, not surprisingly, fairly accurate.

Relax. It doesn't have to be as bad as the horror stories we have heard and can actually serve as good confidence and social skills builders for the kids. The key is to look into activities that *the kids* are interested in, not what *we* think they should be interested in. This is not the time to relive your glory days as the high school quarterback or the first chair tuba player. Allow your child to be an individual and talk to them about what *they* want to try. Mothers shouldn't freak when Janie wants to try hockey and fathers shouldn't spasm when Junior wants to take a cooking class.

Once you've narrowed down an activity, the best place to check is the local paper. Many small town papers, and the community section of larger ones, will list the sports leagues and contact information at the beginning of each season. Begin checking it around the beginning of the school year, again right before Christmas, then around Spring Break and once more before summer vacation starts. You can also look at your local papers online or do a local city search to see if there are any city leagues available.

If your child is interested in music or drama check out the local paper and the bulletin boards in your community. Many times moms with older kids, or even retired people, will offer lessons for children in their home. Of course, you should thoroughly check out the background of anyone with access to your child and never leave them alone.

Finally, check with your local school district. Many of them offer after school enrichment classes at affordable rates. Call your child's school or the local district office if they are not in school yet. Some activities start as young as 2 or 3 years old.

The Bottom Line

Don't put too much stock into finding the *perfect* activity for your kids. Identifying their interests and strengths is done through trial and error. Be willing to help them try a variety of activities. As long as you find something that makes them happy and isn't too much stress on your schedule or budget, go with it. Young children have the attention span of insects and their favorite things will change as frequently as their underwear. One season they may love soccer. By the next, they may want to learn piano, and then by the time school starts they will want to play hockey. Indulge them when you can and if you can't financially swing what they want to do, work together to come up with other options you can more easily afford. Just remember the golden rule of parenting: No matter what activity you find for them, make sure you are all *having fun.*

Chapter 6:
Stuck in the Land of the Little People

It was very hard for me to maintain 'regular' and 'normal' adult interaction, as opposed to my old life when I went to work every day and had daily adult oriented conversations and was free on the weekends to plan outings at the spur of the moment with girl-friends and my husband without having to consider who will take the kids.

- Kelly P., California

Have you ever fancied yourself a recluse? Unless you are willing to put in a little more effort, you could morph into one without even realizing it. While working, unless you had a very isolated job, you were probably forced to talk to at least a few people a day. When you're at home, it becomes much more difficult to get regular adult interaction, especially outside of your immediate family and the cashiers at the local grocery store.

Here are some ways to get a regular adult interaction fix:

• Join a playgroup
• Join an online community for at-home moms or other areas of interest
• Maintain your friendships
• Make new friends.

Playgroups

Ah, the playgroup. As a new SAHM, you may see these as either a mecca or a masochist's dream, an oasis in your parenting desert or a weekly torture chamber. Either way, playgroups and play dates are here to stay. Get used to the idea now and learn to make the most of them…

You've gotta love any event that centers around getting together with other moms, letting the kids play, and then comparing notes about them while they are only two feet away. This is a chance for you to confirm that what you are going through is normal and hear other mom's horror stories which make you feel a little bit better about your own SAHM nightmares. Unfortunately, depending on your playgroup members, it can also be a time for bragging and gloating. If this happens with one of your members, make some lemonade out of the situation and then talk about the "lemon" with the other normal moms once she leaves.

Finding a good playgroup

To make this process as painless as possible, here are some guidelines to finding a playgroup that is a good fit for you and your kids.

1. Look for one close to your house. The less travel time, the better.
2. Seek out one with kids that are the same age as yours. Not only does this help socialize your child, it *really* helps with comparing and competition.
3. Inquire as to what different types of activities the kids in a specific group do.
4. Find out how structured it is. Is it a weekly class with registration dates or just a group of moms who meet at the park?

5. If the group rotates hosting duties, find out what the host is expected to do. You don't want to put even more pressure on yourself by adding a bunch of impossible Martha Stewartesque tasks to your To Do list.

6. Check the local section of our newspaper. Many playgroups will list their meeting times along with the leaders' contact information.

Once you think you have chosen an acceptable playgroup, the next challenge is to see if you can get along with the other moms. Even if your kids love being there, if you can't tolerate the atmosphere it's going to be hell on you each week. You should look forward to hanging with your new friends, not be dreading the witchy mom with the potty mouth.

If you are having trouble finding a playgroup, there are several online resources. One of the biggest is Matching Moms (www.matchingmoms.org). Though not very sophisticated looking, it has listings for playgroups offered all over the country. If you do an online search with your city name and the word playgroup, you may also find some acceptable choices. You can also check My Playgroups (www.myplaygroups.com) to see if there are some groups listed in your area.

It may sound melodramatic, but MOMS Club literally saved my life. After four months on bed rest during my first pregnancy, then another four months being home-bound due to delivery complications, I was desperate for adult interaction. How many times can one read Goodnight Moon to a toddler at ten o'clock in the morning?

I've been in that spot, that edge of the crevasse where sleep depriva-tion and the "give till it hurts" mentality collide with too much time spent looking at the world from the eyes of a small child. And it was my real-life friends, local moms I met through my MOMS Club group, who brought me back from the edge. They were — and sometimes continue to be — my lifeline and I hope, in some way, I am also theirs. We provide each other the context in which we can truly appreciate motherhood and our children as we live our lives with people.

- Sheyna G., Minnesota

Starting your own

If you can't find a playgroup that you like, why not start your own? Here are a few basics you will need to define:

1. What ages will you include?
2. Where will you hold the gatherings?
3. How many kid/mom couples will you include?
4. How often do you want to meet?
5. If you rotate hosts, what is required?

Once you have these basics figured out, the next step is in finding other women to invite. You could go hunt down people at the park — chances are if they are at the park during work hours, they are a SAHM and will welcome the opportunity to be stalked — anything for some adult interaction. But there are many other ways to get the word out.

To find members, you can also try:
   • Posting fliers around your local parks

- Advertising in the local section of the newspaper
- Posting your group information online
- Leaving fliers at your pediatrician's office

Once you have the people signed up, spend some time making sure the inaugural meeting will run smoothly thus insuring your members will be eager for more. The best playgroups are organized, but not overly so. Children are free flow individuals, so have some structured activities available, but mostly provide a clean, organized, SAFE play area where the kids can enjoy themselves with toys, and one another, while their moms vent and enjoy coffee and nibbles a few feet away. Relaxed organization is the key to having a successful playgroup with no cranky kids or cranky moms.

Online communities

Another way to branch out and meet new people is to join and participate in online communities geared towards moms, and more specifically *stay at home* moms. Be warned: the main caveat to online groups is the addiction factor. If you have a tendency to linger online, utilize some of that moderation you use on your children and consider limiting your group participation. The support and friendships you can find online are very real, but the last thing you want to do is let your online time cut into your family time.

When looking for an online community, make sure you invest some time in finding one that fits your needs and personality. There are literally thousands of groups available, so there has to be one out there for you. Try looking for a group based on your location, ethnicity, the age of your kids, favorite hobbies, or even your former career.

Some places to look for online support:
- Babycenter (www.babycenter.com)
- IVillage (www.ivillage.com)
- Yahoo! Groups (www.Yahoo.com)
- Google Groups (www.Google.com)
- MSN Groups (www.groups.msn.com)
- SheKnows (www.talk.sheknows.com)

Maintain Your Friendships

When you become a stay at home mom, the world seems to shrink to a little bubble that surrounds your house and if you don't work to make it bigger, you will be stuck inside it. Maintaining your outside friendships takes more effort, but its worth it. They are your link to the grown up world – a world where people don't talk in rhyme or sing about potty training.

If you have work friendships that you wish to continue, consider setting up a regular happy hour with your business friends. That way you can meet at times which work for them and you can get out the house by yourself.

If you have mom friends you enjoy hanging out with, try setting up a monthly lunch. This way the kids can play in a controlled environment while the moms chat.

The main point to keep in mind is that you protect your social time, that you make it a habit, keep dates on your calendar and realize how very important it is to your well being as a mom.

Make New Friends

If you don't have any friends that are at home with their kids or you don't make an effort to become friends with some at home moms, you will begin to feel isolated pretty quickly. SAH parenting is a lonely job, but the fact is your neighborhood hides dozens of moms just like you – just as isolated and just as desperate for a friendly face that is not covered in fur and living in their TV set. So even if you are shy, you need to make the effort to seek them out.

You've probably heard it before, but it's true: When you have kids, you make most of your adult friends through them. Whether through activities or school, you are sure to make new friends if you just smile and say Hi. I have made quite a few friends through my kid's swimming lessons. The nice thing about making friends at your kid's activities is that you know they have *some* of the same interests as you, *and* if you were to start voicing your opinions about the difficulties of staying home, you are guaranteed to find at least one, if not half, of the moms in attendance echoing the same sentiments. There *is* strength in numbers.

So look around when you are out with your kids. If you happen to see the same mom at the park every day, ask if she wants to come over for snack. Even if a friendship doesn't work out, at least the kids can play together.

The Bottom Line

Having friends who understand what you are going through as an at-home mom is going to be very important to your survival…sorry, I mean *adjustment,* in your new role in life. Even if you are shy, force yourself to make the effort to find other women who know what it's like to be a SAHM. There will be days when you need a sympathetic ear willing to listen to you whine in order to keep your sanity. Plus, the more friends you have for support and companionship, the happier and more confident you will become. Your kids will notice. Your husband will notice. And most importantly, YOU will notice.

SECTION 3
The Logistics of It All

Chapter 7:
How Much Is A Housekeeper?

Chapter 8:
Family Management

Chapter 9:
You Mean, You're Not Betty Crocker?

Chapter 10:
Money, Or Lack Thereof

Chapter 7:
How Much Is A Housekeeper?

If it's really important to you that your family help keep the house clean and organized, but they don't want to, try every means at your disposal. If none of them work, trade in your family for a cleaner one. - Sherri M., North Carolina

Now that you are a SAHM, there is an enormous amount of pressure on you to manage the household. Couple that with the enormous amount of pressure you are already placing on yourself and you can begin to feel just as overwhelmed as inadequate. First, we have women like Martha Stewart telling us how our house "should" look. Get over "shoulds" now. Martha Stewart has a cadre of underlings who keep her abodes and commodes sparkling and pristine.

Then we have all these preconceived notions about what a SAHM does and what she should accomplish. As I said before, you cannot fully appreciate the job of SAHM until you are doing it and when it comes to housework, there is one defining principle to keep in mind: Don't let it consume your life. You are not staying home to be a maid (feel free to tell your husband I said this). Your days will not contain enough time to polish your teeth, let alone your silver. The iron will become a giant paperweight and any item of clothing that requires its heat will be left on the rack in the store. You will cultivate a new form of cleaning called "closing the bedroom doors". Plain and simple, you are staying home to raise your children, so practice this mantra...ready? "I am not a maid. I am not a maid. I am not a maid." Repeat it whenever the dust bunnies are competing against your children for your attention. Say it aloud when your husband dares to mention the piles of debris around the hacienda. Tack it to the refrigerator door and read it three times whenever you feel guilt begin to creep in over preparing yet another box of Macaroni -n- Cheese.

Now, even though we have established that you are *not* a maid, you will still want to have some semblance of order in your house. Remember, this was easier when no one was in it during the days. Suddenly though, you will notice within about two days of staying home that your house seems smaller. Obviously it's not, but the piles reduce the floor space and emotionally it may feel like the walls are closing in. Those walls will recede as you adapt, but the floor space will remain an issue. Remember, you are now home *all the time.* This means you and your kids have *all the time* to make *all the messes.* The key to the clutter is to find your own level of comfort. Some people need to have a spotless house to feel comfortable (personally I think they are sick in the head). Others, including myself, have come to terms with a certain allotment of clutter.

Just as you are not a maid, being home all the time does not mean you should be the only one insuring that the house presentable. *You all live there.* This means you must talk to your husband and kids and determine just how to break up household tasks so everyone is contributing and no one is overwhelmed. For some, this means splitting things evenly; others may feel like picking up more of the workload. As your children get a bit older — preschool/Kindergarten age — they should be expected to help more and begin taking on additional tasks. By that age they are certainly old enough to make a mess and they are certainly old enough to help clean it back up. This is not mean, this is teaching them responsibility and accountability.

Having been a family full of people who have all been away during the days, don't expect miracles once you inform everyone of the new rules and their new roles. It will take time for the family to get used to the new plan, *but they need to get used to it.* In the beginning you should consider it a work in progress and expect to alter it many times. Eventually everyone *will* settle in and you will all be working like a finely oiled machine — one that may require tinkering from time to time, but one that is built to last.

Remember, developing a plan of attack helps — it shows that you are at least making an attempt to keep order amidst the chaos.

Getting It All Done — *Housework*

I don't know too many moms who enjoy doing housework. Come to think of it, I don't know any and if I did, I would seriously worry about them. Housework is one of the least enjoyable tasks for a SAHM. But like many things in life, it is a necessary evil. Not only does a moderately organized, slightly hygienic house up the comfort level for everyone who lives there, maintaining it is a perfect example to set for young children.

Whether you share 1,000 square feet or 10,000 square feet, breaking housecleaning tasks into smaller projects can make it go a little easier. It also fits better into a schedule dominated by children. It is much more reasonable to plan on cleaning the bathrooms one day, the kitchen the next, dusting another day, etc, as opposed to trying to clean your house top to bottom in one day. Some people enjoy cleaning as a family on the weekends, but personally I prefer to spend that time hanging out with my husband and the kids, not cleaning toilets and baseboards.

Make sure the schedule you create works for you and is flexible. If it isn't working, change it. If something comes up and you can't get to "Vacuum Under Couch" on its specified day, don't sweat it. The dust bunnies are perfectly happy and will wait for you. I have been home for several years now and I am constantly changing the way I do things. I also have days, and even weeks, where I don't stick to my schedule. There is no perfect science to cleaning a house and each week is different. For example, if your child is sick, your time is much better invested in reading them a book and snuggling, than in reorganizing your hall closet. Remember, it's the thought that counts. That phrase may not have been meant for this situation, but it certainly applies. Here's one of the many weekly schedules I have tried:

Monday - Clean up from the weekend.

Tuesday - Laundry, vacuum living room.

Wednesday - My room & bathrooms.

Thursday - Laundry, vacuum living room.

Friday - Clean up for weekend.

Every day I clean the kitchen (counters, table, dishes, sink). I also fit in cleaning the kids' rooms whenever possible. You might notice that I don't have "cleaning my kids' bathroom" on this list. One of the most helpful time saving tips I have learned is to clean the kids' bathroom while they are taking a bath. You can only do this when they are a little older and you have to prepare everything before you get them in the bath, but mirrors, sinks and toilets can easily be washed down while the kids are splashing away. Just be safe and make sure you don't leave the chemicals in the bathroom.

Make a plan. Don't try to do it all at one time. I clean one room each day and pick up common areas each day. Don't let it overwhelm you. Do what you can and remember that a little dust never killed anyone!   - Lee Ann S., Missouri

Husbands and Housework

I've said it before and I will say it again — *you are not at home to be a maid.* This huge misconception is typically held by most husbands of new SAHM's. They have no concept of what you actually do during the day and mistakenly assume the house should be spotless and dinner made when they arrive home, like some 50s flashback of Ozzie & Harriet. Do not let this mindset take root in your home because once it does, it is a very hard one to dig out. From the first day you stay home, his *not* helping should *not* even be an option. Talk with your husband about what he is going to do to help around the house. He lives there and it is just as much his responsibility as yours. Mention that his proactive assistance will not only leave you more energy for the evenings, but will ensure resentment stays at bay, thus insuring a much more pleasant environment for everyone. Your family will quickly learn that if you are happy, everyone is happy, and they will see the wisdom is pitching in.

When you split up the household tasks, don't underestimate his ability to do certain things, but do try to give him tasks at which he can succeed. Sure, you may need to lower your standards and bite your tongue as you watch him do *his* chores *his* way, but it will be worth it. If you give him tasks and then nag him, he will invariably shut down and not want to help. Men are very black and white creatures — they do not think in terms of gray areas, so if you need something done in a specific way, tell him. Do not just say, "Clean the bathroom." That is too vague. Simply explain, "Honey, can you wipe down the counters, Windex the mirror, use the Scrubbing Bubbles under the sink on the tub, and shake the bathmats off outside? Thanks." Being specific ensures his success and when you praise him afterwards, you will both feel great. Positive reinforcement goes a long way and will be a welcome alternative to stereotypical wife nagging.

I always thought it so unfair that my husband would come home from work and collapse on the couch or do emails or watch TV while I cooked dinner, cleared the table, got the baby ready for bed, and then did bottles, diapers and whatever. Maybe I didn't have a paying "real" job but I sure didn't sit on my butt all day. When I told him how exhausted I was and complained that moms can't punch a time clock the way he did, he understood and we decided to take turns. He would have his down time before and immediately after dinner and then we split up evening duties and alternated every other night. That way it got done quicker and I got to sit down sooner, but mainly he didn't feel harassed and I didn't feel resentful. He's always been great about doing his share around the house but just needed to be told.

-Hannah H., Illinois

It's Not All About You (This Time): Letting the Little Ones Help

One of the biggest points I can stress about housework is this: enlist help. Most of us cannot afford to hire a housekeeper, although we *can* dream, can't we? No, I am suggesting that, as with your husband, you enlist your family's help. Remember our new mantra? There is no reason that you can't get even the youngest kids involved in the process. I had my son start helping when he was about 2; now he knows he is expected to pitch in. It's not always helpful, but he *is* trying and it lays the groundwork for when he is older and can begin relieving my husband and I of some of our duties.

One of the easiest (and safest) ways to get younger kids involved starts with cleaning the living room. Typically this includes vacuuming, dusting, wiping off tables, etc. Little ones can easily help pick up toys to clear the floor for vacuuming. If they are too little to do this by themselves, walk around the room with them with a storage bucket and let them put the toys in there. This makes it more of a game, which translates to fun for them. Sure it will take a little longer, but you will be spending quality time with them and teaching, at least in theory, that the toys do not pick themselves up and that they do, in fact, have the ability to pick up after themselves.

Another way to involve them is with the dusting. I use cheap diaper wipes to dust the living room. Since they are safe for kids to use with supervision, I let my kids "dust" anything within arm's reach (with the exception of things like the TV screen). Diaper wipes also work well for wiping down tables and walls (and are excellent for a quick freshen up-spot cleaning of your own self before hubby comes home!).

In the kitchen, kids can pitch in in several ways. Younger kids can help set and clear the table as long as you only let them handle non-breakables, unless of course, you are vying for a new china set. Kids as young as two can help put dishes in the dishwasher. They are also good at replenishing napkins and paper towels when needed. Other tasks they can master are holding the dustpan while you sweep the floor, putting a new bag in the trash can and wiping down the table after meals. Smaller children love to be given a damp rag or baby wipe and let loose to "clean" the lower cabinets. Shy away from sponges as tiny tots may chew off a piece.

Kids' Bedrooms

Cleaning kids' bedrooms can either be a cake walk or a complete nightmare. When it comes to most kids' rooms it's often a combination of both. Try to make it easy for kids to pick up by themselves. If you try to enforce a rigid routine, it most likely won't work. If you have expectations that are too high for them, you are setting both of you up for failure. Clearly explain what is expected of them. Just as with your husband, saying "Clean your room" is incredibly vague and frustrating for them. Besides, our idea of clean, even if it is very relaxed, is still vastly different from our kid's idea of clean. Tell them the specifics involved, from picking up all the toys on the floor to dusting their dressers to arranging their shoes in the closet.

Of course, the easiest way to help your children keep their room clean would be to get rid of all of their toys. Since this isn't a viable option, we are forced to come up with other ways to help them out. I strongly recommend that you do not use a traditional toy box in which to store their toys. The Murphy's Law of toy boxes dictates that all the good toys will somehow sift down to the bottom and when they can't find what they are looking for, they will just dump the entire box. If you use some version of a storage bin system, at least when they dump out the contents of the box to look for something, there is less to dump, ergo less to clean. Try to arrange the room for optimum kid effectiveness. If it is difficult in any way, shape, or form for kids to put something away, they won't. When my husband moved my son's bookshelf to a different corner of his room, he suddenly forgot how to put any books back on the shelf. I moved the shelf and he has regained his ability to put his books away. It all goes back to KISS-Keep It Simple Sister. And remember to heap on the positive reinforcement.

Laundry

How long did it take you to feel like you were washing not only your family's clothes, but your neighbor's clothes too? When you stay home full time, there is a lot more time to get clothes dirty and the laundry grows exponentially. With messy arts and crafts supplies being flung about and food and drinks being spilled all the time, you will be washing everyone's clothes – constantly. You would do well to invest in a laundry detergent stock now. Surely the dividends will cover your retirement.

Surprisingly, this *is* another domestic task that you can have the kids help with. Younger children can easily put their clothes in a clothes basket or hamper; just make sure it's easily accessible. Kids also like helping with the actual washing process. Face it, anything that has buttons *and* water *must* be cool. So give them the responsibility to put the clothes in the dryer. You place the wet items in a plastic hamper, insuring nothing goes in that shouldn't, and then they empty that hamper into the dryer. They can also push baskets to and from the laundry room, and even take freshly dried clothes out of the dryer and into a basket to move it to the appropriate room in the house. This is not child labor. You are reinforcing good habits, teaching them responsibility and they will feel trusted and valuable to the whole process.

You may not like the results when your kids help with the laundry, but remember — perfection is overrated. It doesn't need to be perfect and there are other ways to do things besides your way. If the socks are in the wrong drawer or the shirts are hung up inside out, no big deal. If your kids see you going behind them and fixing everything they've done, they will feel judged and tested and won't want to help anymore. Relax your standards and find something else to worry about – there's plenty of other choices.

Not being a big fan of doing laundry, my washing schedule usually varies from week to week. After using Mondays to recover from the weekend, I use the middle days of the week to tackle the fabric mountains. One week I might attempt a marathon washing session and get it all done in one day. Other weeks I take a few extra days to complete the loads. As long as everyone has clean underwear, the rest can wait.

Here is another confession: I don't always put the clothes away immediately and I *never* iron. When you have two little ones, it can sometimes be next to impossible to prioritize time during the day for such mundane tasks. Sometimes, I let the clean clothes sit in the laundry basket and simply pull out items we need, as we need them. Scandalous, isn't it? And some of you might be wondering how I get away without ironing. Well, one, I don't really care if there are a few wrinkles on our clothes because chances are they will get wrinkled anyway when wearing a seatbelt, so why waste my time? Two, if something is wrinkled, just spray it with a water bottle and hang it up in the shower — most of the wrinkles will fall right out. If it is really bad, put it in the dryer for a few minutes with a damp towel and no more wrinkles! For dress clothes, you can check to see if your dryer has an "air only" cycle. The clothes can be thrown in with a damp towel and no heat so you don't have to worry about shrinking them. Keep it simple and be willing to improvise.

The Bottom Line

Cleaning and maintaining a house is a gargantuan task. Pair this with raising your kids and it can seem insurmountable. Always remind yourself that you are not staying home in order to have an immaculate house; you are there for your kids. Don't let cleaning the house get in the way of being with them. Make sure you enlist the help you need from your husband and kids. Involve everyone. Again, *you all live there. The messes belong to everyone, therefore, everyone should be expected to pitch in.* Allowing them to view you as their servant, even for one day, pretty much guarantees you will have to resort to drastic measures down the road. But really, is threatening to go on strike or constantly nagging your husband about how much a housekeeper costs *really* how you want to live? How *any* of you wants to live? Start on day one and they will realize you are serious. Strive for a balance that works for *your family.* Don't worry about what the neighbors do, what your sister does, how your mom did it. What matters is what works under your roof. Chores may never completely equal out (I mean we *are* moms after all), but at least you won't feel like you have to do everything all the time.

Chapter 8:
Family Management — Surviving Day To Day Life

Surviving the day to day tasks of an at home mom requires three integral traits — boatloads of patience, the ability to plan, and an additional Titanic sized portion of patience (no, there isn't a fourth category for margaritas). Ironically, staying on top of things as a working mom was easier, essentially because we were forced to be organized. With all those balls in the air, you know — all the comings and goings, and job, family and extracurricular commitments — it was an organizational sink or swim. Suddenly, now that your day is no longer divided into clearly marked segments and obligations, there is more time for things to slip through the cracks. It's not that you're less busy — in fact, you are more busy than before — but the busy-ness is less defined, more scattered and abstract. Essentially, as a working mom, your life resembled a Picasso during his Cubist period. As a stay at home mom, your life is more akin to a Jackson Pollack splash and smear canvas. No less valuable, just a very different utilization and interpretation of talent.

But like the frenzied speckles and splotches in Pollack's masterpieces, your life at home can quickly spiral out of control. This is why it's important to institute a routine and adopt a weekly plan. Sure, your canvas will still lean towards the abstract, but you will know that there is rhyme and reason, even if the outside world still sees only dollops and dashes of "paint".

Schedule, We Don't Need No Stinkin' Schedule

Yes, I do realize that you thought that since you were no

longer working at a regular J.O.B. you would never again be constrained by a schedule. I know you envisioned placid days that would ebb and flow like a peaceful summer tide. That you'd just live one day to the next, in the moment, like some watercolor portrait come to life. I hate to burst your bubble, but living like that is only suitable for brief tropical vacations when Grandma is at home watching the kids. In your real life, having a schedule might not make your new at home world very glamorous, but it will make your day to day existence much smoother. Face it, human beings are creatures of habit and find comfort in set routines. Even if you are the creative type who thinks schedules are only for tightly wound Type A's, you will still benefit.

Since you are used to being at work, you can incorporate work place strategies to help get your home organized. Remember, you are the CEO of the house (a title that may or may not have changed since you've been home). One of the main systems you can implement is the weekly schedule. Don't panic — I'm not suggesting anything maximum-security-prison-inflexible; flexibility is a key trait to have as a stay at home mom. What I am suggesting is creating some sort of daily schedule that provides your week with some structure. This will prevent the days from blending together and gives you a much better shot at staying on top of everything.

When you are creating your schedule, you first need to take into account the activities that are set in stone, such as classes for the kids, sports practices and any other activities you are committed to on a regular basis. You *do* have activities planned that are just for *you* on a regular basis, right? If not, *immediately* refer to the chapter about taking care of yourself. That's an order.

The next factors to take into account are your good and bad days. For example, I am not a Monday person. After the weekend, I need to have time to get the house back in order from my husband being home all weekend and the various activities we do; therefore I do a general cleaning on Mondays and pick up any clutter and random dishes left over from the weekend. I also use Monday to ease myself back into the week. Even though you're not at work, you'll probably find that you still need a day to recover from the weekends. Remember, "work" for you no longer stops at 5pm on a Friday. You are on duty, 24/7/365, ma'am.

Calendars = Scheduled Chaos

Think back to when you were working and the buzz was about time management and being effective. You can use those same principles to help you organize your family. It is essential that you use some type of calendar to get and stay organized. It should be the first thing you look at in the morning and the last thing you look at before going to bed. First, you need to decide what type of calendar you prefer. Some moms use a very basic calendar that fits in their purse. While handy, these don't really allow you to record enough information. Many moms prefer a calendar with large date squares so they have plenty of room to write down appointments, play dates, phone numbers, etc. Still others use very elaborate systems, including items like address books, places to keep notes, shopping lists and several loads of laundry. Some people are even comfortable using PDAs. Whatever you decide to go with, get a system that allows you room for additional information, such as business cards, phone

numbers and gift idea lists. You will appreciate this extra convenience when you are out at the store and need a size or you're at
the doctor and you need your insurance company's information.

Whatever your poison, I mean choice, you have to commit
to using it on a regular basis. A system is no good if you don't take
advantage of it.

Now, with calendar in hand, enter all of your regular activities. I recommend writing everything down in pencil. That way
if you need to change anything — and you know you will — you
can do so and still have a relatively neat looking calendar. Once
you have done that, sit back and look at the time you have left
and think about your prime days. Now you can work on creating
your weekly schedule. Remember, your weekly schedule includes
activities for you and the kids. You may or may not want to put
your home cleaning schedule on your calendar. I don't do this,
just because it would cause me more stress to see all the stuff I'm
not doing. Instead, I created a weekly task list that I post by my
computer and my fridge. This way, it reminds me of all the things
I "should" be doing when I am wasting time surfing the net or
getting the kids a snack.

Now you have a calendar with the entire family's schedules
and your master weekly schedule. What more could there possibly be? Well, now you need to make sure you have a calendar with
you at all times. So if you have chosen to use a big, wall style calendar for your schedule, you will also need to get a smaller purse
sized version. Having a calendar with you at all times will help
you in two ways. One, it will prevent you from writing appointments and other important dates on little slips of paper while
you are out and about, and two, it will prevent you from forget-

ting important activities because you lost those little slips of paper. Do not write stuff down on sticky notes to add to your calendar later. How many times has one of your kids taken off with, colored on or tried to eat a sticky note? Exactly.

While we are discussing having your calendar with you at all times, there is some other information that you should always have with you as well. If you choose to use a planner system or PDA, it will be easy to keep all of this with you. This information includes:

• Phone numbers to doctor's offices, for both you and your kids.

• Your kids' social security numbers.

• Phone numbers to your local pharmacy and to a 24 hour pharmacy.

• Phone number to a potential babysitter if you have one available.

• Phone number to your car insurance agent.

• Phone number for a tow truck company (for those who can't change a tire).

Easy access to this information will make your life easier, I guarantee it. If you need to call the doctor with an emergency while at a play date, you will have all of the necessary information at hand. Nothing makes a stressful situation more stressful like having to leaf through an out of date Yellow Pages — you need your information to be readily available.

Errands — Living Life in the Minivan

Now that you are at home, you will have the pleasure of running most, if not all, of the family errands. If at all possible, make a plan for this, especially if your kids are younger. If your kids are in school, obviously you can run errands while they are gone. If you have a toddler or baby, you will want to keep the errand running under control, or you risk turning your little angel into a temper tantrum throwing tyrant.

Here's a few ways to make errands less painful:

1. Errand Days - Pick a few days a week to run errands and try to stick to those days when possible. If your kids know what to expect, it can make the irritation of being in the car less so.

2. Plan Ahead - On errand days, pack snacks, drinks and portable activities for the kids' entertainment. Some of our popular items include crayons, pens and pencils with an assortment of little notebooks. Kids can "write" their own stories, color, practice letter writing, etc.

3. Don't Mess with Naptime - If at all possible, don't let errand running interfere with naptime. Naptime should be guarded, protected and revered. It is a part of your child's routine, which plays into their feelings of safety and security and it is your guaranteed quite time in the day. Even if you have to split the errands between the morning and afternoon or two different days, this is a much better alternative than having a tired and cranky kid in the middle of a grocery store or mall or a child who has slept sideways in his car seat for thirty miles.

4. Keep it Fun - Kids do not like running errands. Sure, they may be excited at first, but it usually wears off about 3 minutes after getting to your first destination. If you can make a game out of it (play I Spy in the grocery store) or get them involved (make them your big helper

and let them hold the list if they won't eat it), outings can be accomplished under the guise of having fun.

5. Be Patient - I realize I just said this, but kids do not like running errands. They will get cranky, they will not listen and they will try your patience. Errands are not about them or anything that even remotely interests them, so there is really nothing for them to do but vent their frustration, boredom and inconvenience. Keep this in mind and keep the upper hand by staying calm. Resolve to not get into a screaming match and do not play into tantrums. Getting mad and having a meltdown in the middle of the store won't benefit either of you.

How to Get Things Done Around the House

Unless you are nocturnal and require little sleep, you will need to find ways to get everything done during the day. Whether it's cleaning the floors or cooking a meal, trying to accomplish your tasks with kids underfoot can be next to impossible. I know I am banging this drum again, but **have a plan**. If you have ideas in place to deal with the kids when they are swinging from the ceiling fans while you are trying not to burn dinner, you can effectively deal with the situation instead of exploding.

It may sound counterintuitive, but the best way to get the kids out of your hair is to get them involved. Ignoring them or shunting them to the side only increases their desire to get your attention in any way possible. But if you can incorporate them into the process, it suddenly becomes fun and a sense of team spirit takes over. Redirecting their energy allows you to work through your To-Do list and make them feel involved. Sure, sometimes it may be necessary to take more drastic measures and engage them in a movie or extra cartoon, and that's perfectly fine. If you need to make a bathroom run, pay the bills, wrap a gift, or return an important call, this can buy you the 10 - 15 minutes you need to get finished.

Quick Ways to Occupy the Kidlets:

1. Give them bowls and spoons and let them cook up a feast with their imaginations.

2. Let them color with chalk or markers or regular pens (anything away from the norm). Just be sure you provide paper or your walls could take on that Jackson Pollack look.

3. Let them help set the table. Who cares if the forks are upside down and where the spoons belong? Kids learn by doing.

4. Have them create a menu for the meal. Give them ownership of a task — it is wonderful for their self confidence.

5. Let them help with the prep work. If you are making snack, let them get the plates and bowls. If you are making dinner, let them carry stuff from the fridge to the counter.

6. If you are trying to clean something, give the kids a small portion of it as their responsibility. A wet cloth or paper towel is all it takes.

7. While cleaning, make it a race to see who can complete their task the quickest. Suddenly it's not a chore, it's a game!

8. Put on a movie. Again, this is perfectly fine. Moderation is the key to anything, so as long as they are not living in front of the rectangular nanny or watching Freddie Kruger on Elm Street, a movie treat is a good thing.

9. Have them read a book to you while you work. They learn and entertain at the same time.

10. Keep a special toy, activity or book for times when you need to get something accomplished (this works great when you are on the phone or trying to use the bathroom without the kids watching).

11. See if they can complete a puzzle before you finish your task. Just don't cheat and give them one of those 4,000 piece, 3-D puzzles — you're not cleaning the Sistine Chapel, you know.

12. Let them cut pictures out of a magazine. Turn it into a scavenger hunt by giving them a list of pictures to find.

13. Let them play an age appropriate computer game. Face it, computers are their future. By the time they are in second grade they will be creating their own Power Point presentations in school, so expose them to the keyboard early.

14. Let them play video games while you complete what you need to do. Like TV, a romp with Mario will not burn their brain cells when played in moderation.

15. Send them on an impromptu scavenger hunt throughout the house. Winner gets to choose dessert.

16. Ball up some computer paper and let them have a snowball fight. Let them create "snow forts" out of sheets and furniture.

17. Tie a towel around their necks and let them be a super-
hero. It's Wamsutta Man! Able to dry small bottoms in a
single wipe!

18. Give them some empty boxes and let them play store.
This one never goes out of style — kids LOVE anything
that allows them to mimic the grown-up world they see.

The Bottom Line

The day to day life of an at home mom can become tedious and chaotic without proper planning. Develop a schedule and use a calendar to keep the bedlam at bay, or to at least know when it's coming. Plan ahead for the times you need to clean up for an impending houseguest or just to make the daily snack. If you approach your daily tasks with a plan in mind, you will minimize the potential for chaos. Let me rephrase that — you will still have the chaos, but what you will cut down on is the potential for a Mommy blow up.

Chapter 9:
You Mean, You're Not Betty Crocker?

I didn't know you were supposed to rinse out chickens.

I am known as the family's worst cook. This fact was con-firmed one day when I attempted to cook a nice, wholesome, seemingly easy meal for my family. My husband pulled out a whole roasting chicken for dinner that night. He gave me the cooking instructions several times: put the seasonings on, cut up potatoes and carrots, throw it all in a baking pan, and cook it for about an hour and a half.

"I got it. I got it. I'm not stupid, I can follow simple instructions," I huffed after my husband reconfirmed the direc-tions with me for the fourth time that day.

When it came time to prepare the meal, I seasoned the chicken, cut up the veggies, put it all in a baking pan, and put it in the oven to bake. I checked its progress over the next hour and a half, and while it seemed to be cooking slowly, it was progress-ing. And he thought I couldn't follow directions.

When my husband got home from work, he commented on how good the house smelled. And when he opened the oven, he gave me a impressed glance. "Wow, that looks really good." He then pulled the chicken out to make sure it was done. Then he cut into it...

"It's still frozen."

"What?!? It can't be. I cooked it for almost 2 hours."

"Did you rinse it out before you seasoned it?"

I laughed. Then I realized that he wasn't kidding.

"Alana, you didn't clean out the chicken before you cooked it?"

I looked at him like he was crazy. "Why would I need to rinse out a chicken? Isn't it ready to cook when you buy it?"

My husband huffed. He took the chicken out of the oven, and proceeded to pull out the chicken's still frozen giblet pack.

Needless to say, we had pizza for dinner that night.

Let Them Eat

Cooking meals for the family on a regular basis can be an intimidating task. You have to plan the meal, get the shopping done, then prepare the meal and clean up afterwards (although quite frankly, the clean-up should be delegated to the husband — share in those chores, remember, you are not a maid, you are not a maid...). Many moms think that when they stay home, they will have time to do things as outlandish as baking bread from scratch and serving meals with multiple courses. Dreamers.

Imagine their disappointment when reality hits. How many moms are willing, much less able, to cook a full meal after chasing around one or more kids all day? I realize that there are those mutant moms out there who somehow accomplish this feat on a regular basis, but they are also the same ones who always have a spotless house and brag about it during their kids' classes. Makes me believe there *are* aliens among us.

You Can't Burn Boiled Water

The only way for you to learn how to cook regularly is to roll up your sleeves and try. I understand how scary this is for many women. There have been many nights when I have "tried." Unfortunately, many of these nights I have also ended up calling my husband and asking him to pick up dinner on the way home.

Michelle Stern, a Pampered Chef consultant and owner of What's Cooking (www.whatscooking.com), suggests new at home moms "sit back, take a breath and think about what you are afraid of. Then, look up some simple recipes on the internet and TRY them! The worst thing that can happen is that you burn your food...the best thing that can happen is that you increase your self esteem and succeed."

Luckily, there *are* easy ways to get food on the table. They are not necessarily going to fit with the latest diet trend, nor are they gourmet in any sense of the word, but your meals will still be edible. The basic premise to keep in mind is that there are three segments to a family meal: a meat, a side, and a veggie. Later I will list some basic staples to have on hand to help you break out of this pattern, but this is a good place to start.

Meats

Most of us being carnivores, let's start with meats. You will need to decide what your comfort level is in terms of handling and cooking different types. I have no problem cooking hamburger or pork, but for some reason I get nervous when faced with a chicken and I don't even attempt to cook steak. Try to find a few different meats that you are comfortable working with (stop snickering), which will usually be defined as the meats you have not incinerated or ruined previously, then you can branch out later. If you aren't comfortable with any type, I suggest you try starting with hamburger and pork chops. They are both easy to work with and beginner-friendly.

There are some basic points about cooking meat you must keep in mind. First, if it is frozen, remember to defrost it. Sounds silly, but how many times have you wanted to cook something in particular only to discover it was still locked in an Arctic deep freeze? The easiest way to handle this is to either take something out each morning or take something out for the next day after you finish dinner. If you have 24 hours, place the frozen meat in the refrigerator. If you choose to defrost it on the counter, do not leave it out all day — bacteria will grow. Also, most microwave ovens have defrost settings on them, but like VCR clocks, no one ever bothered to read the manual to know how to set them. Get yours out and learn how to use the feature on your microwave — it can save you in a defrosting pinch.

When you are cooking meat you also need to follow proper meat handling guidelines (what did I say about snickering?). Above all else, make sure you wash your hands and any surfaces thoroughly after they come into contact with any meat. This is especially true for chicken and pork. Eschew wood cutting boards as bacteria can seep into the grains. Plastic or glass cutting boards are ideal since they do not absorb the inevitable juices. Not following this simple rule could cause someone in the family to get very sick and we already have enough guilt to deal with.

Now that you know which meat you feel comfortable with, and you know how to "handle" it, how will you cook it? For the beginning cook, the choices are overwhelming; should you grill, bake, fry, sear, sauté, broil, crock pot, boil, blanch, stir fry, roast, steam, or braise? Don't fret if you don't recognize some of these terms — I didn't either! I list them to illustrate that you have plenty of choices and to encourage you to begin watching the Food Network. A few weeks with Emeril, Rachel Ray, the Barefoot Contessa, and a couple Iron Chef episodes and you'll be a pro in no time.

Next, you need to season the meat. This can be difficult for a beginner because how do you know how much seasoning to put on? Some people just "know" when to stop. I am not one of those. I am more likely to look at what I have seasoned and judge by how much of the meat is still visible. Just so you know, this is not necessarily the best method. The point to keep in mind is that you can always *add* more seasoning, but it is much harder to *get rid* of too much seasoning (unless you rinse it off, which I have done many, many times). And always go easy on salt which tends to dry meat out. Let each person add to their own taste once it is on their plate.

Here are some basic seasonings to keep on hand:
• Lawry's Season Salt
• Tabasco Sauce
• Any of Emeril's seasonings
• Garlic Powder (be careful if you use garlic salt, it is NOT the same thing and it is very easy to use too much)
• Lawry's Perfect Blends
• McCormick's Montreal Steak Seasoning
• McCormick's Mesquite Chicken Seasoning
• Lemon Pepper
• Bay Leaves
• Italian Seasoning
• Oregano
• Parsley

There are plenty of others you can add to this list, but these are some basic ones to get you started.

Sides

Here's where it gets easy to be a bit less creative. The problem (or solution, depending on how you look at it) is that there are so many side dish choices that don't require any thought on your part. You can buy rice, potatoes of practically any kind, and pastas all conveniently waiting for you in a box or bag — just zap in your microwave.

Some people are really against using prepared side items. They don't like the sodium content or they don't like that they can't pronounce half of the ingredients or they feel like less of a cook for taking the easy way out. While this is a valid concern — "prepared" is pretty synonymous with "preservatives" and "processed", the way I see it, these are foods that I can easily prepare, are really, really difficult to mess up, and which I know, for the most part, will be edible. What more can I ask than that? It still beats take out, it's cheaper and I can at least feel like I prepared *something*.

Thinking Outside the Box (and Bag)

If you are feeling really feisty or you want to really impress your family by cooking a side item that you don't dump out of a package first, there are a few really good options out there, including potatoes, pastas and rice.

Potatoes

Potatoes give a beginner or time crunched cook some very good options. You can do all of the following quite easily:

• *Microwave baked* - Most microwaves even have a specific button that reads "Potatoes". To make them come out even more like real oven baked potatoes, my husband swears by placing them in a wet paper towel first. I still worry about it short circuiting the microwave, but it hasn't happened yet and they really do come out better this way.

• *Baked in the oven* - 400 degrees for about 45 minutes to an hour - poke with a fork to test tenderness. Depending on how ambitious you are feeling, you can bake them once or twice (twice baked potatoes are great during the winter). You can also add a veggie and sauce on top and eat them as a full meal (broccoli and cheese are particular faves in my house). This is a great way to disguise veggies from picky eaters.

• *Fried on the stove* - Having a grandmother of German descent, this was one of my favorite meals growing up. Slice them up and fry them in oil (blot them with a paper towel first or the potato liquid may splatter hot oil), sprinkle with some Lawry's and salt, then place them on a paper towel to soak up some of the grease before serving.

• *Cut up and baked in the oven* - To really impress someone, cut potatoes (sweet potatoes for an extra gourmet twist) into small chunks, toss them with a little bit of olive oil, sprinkle them with rosemary or your favorite seasonings, and bake them in a 400 degree oven until they are soft.

Rice

This is another side item that is practically impossible to mess up, unless you cook it too long, which in case you hadn't already noticed, messes up just about anything you cook. With rice, you can:

• *Microwave it* - I can only eat it this way with lots of sugar, but some like it with a little butter or margarine, salt and pepper.

• *Microwave with soup or bouillon* - if you want the rice to actually have some flavor, cook it with a can of soup or some beef or chicken bouillon. When I say soup, I am referring to Cream of … whatever your tastes are. You probably don't want to cook rice with alphabet soup or clam chowder (of course, kids have been known to eat stranger things).

• *Oven* - if you put it in a baking pan with a can of soup and some chicken and veggies, you will have an entire meal ready with little prep in about an hour. Check out the inside labels of your soup cans for great recipes.

Pasta

Pasta is another versatile, easy to make side dish. Some people tend to jazz it up with meats and veggies, turning it a main dish, but if you use a prepared sauce, you instantly have a simple side dish. Pasta preparations can include:

• Prepared sauce, topped with a little cheese for an instant side dish. A classic Italian twist? Simply toss pasta with a little olive oil and fresh basil.

• Bake cooked pasta with a red sauce and chicken breasts, top with cheese for Chicken Parmesan.

• Cut up meat and veggies and mix in with the sauce and noodles for an easy main dish.

Vegetables

I love cooking veggies because once you get them figured out they're something you can rely on. What's even better about vegetables is their versatility. Hot or cold, sauced or plain, you can make endless types of salads for both side dishes and main courses. Plus they up the health ante in your meals.

I love my microwave. This is the absolute easiest way to cook veggies. Sure you can use the stove, but it's usually less messy to cook in the microwave and I am all for having less dishes to clean. If the veggies are from a can, just throw them in a bowl and cook them for a few minutes. One of the best products I have incorporated into my kitchen is a microwavable vegetable steamer. Steaming veggies is a wonderful way to consistently eat fresh vegetables and with a microwave steamer, just put water in the bottom, throw in the veggies and a few minutes later they are ready to eat.

If you don't have a steamer for the microwave, you can buy a cheap one that fits inside a sauce pan. You can even create a steam effect by balling up aluminum foil and placing it in the bottom of the pot, over the water, and placing the vegetables on top. Just be sure to check your pans manuals first to make sure you won't mess up their finish.

Cooking On a Regular Basis

I have always considered getting dinner on the table regularly a major accomplishment. (Still do.) It seems like my children always need me most when I'm up to my elbows in raw meat.
- Shelly W., Ohio

Knowing how to cook is one thing; doing it on a regular basis is quite another (just ask any married man). The key is planning. It may seem a little nerdy, even anal, at first, but take some time at the beginning of each week to plan what you will make. Even if you give yourself the leeway to decide which day you will make which meal, it will eliminate most of the guess work when you're asked, "Mooooom, what's for dinner?" You can simply consult your list, pull out the items you need, and cook away.

Stern recommends doubling your recipes so you have built-in leftovers for lunch or dinner the next day. "For example, if you double the amount of pasta and chicken one day, you can make a stir fry that night, and use the remaining chicken and pasta for ingredients for a salad the next day. It takes you the same amount of time to cook a whole bag of pasta as it does half, yet it saves you the time of getting out the pot, filling it with water and waiting for it boil a second time."

To take this a step further, you can have theme nights. With this system, each night of the week has a theme and the meal for that night revolves around it. For example, if Tuesday is Mexican night, one week you may have Enchiladas, while the next Tuesday you have Chicken Taco Salads. Make it fun and involve the family in selecting the nightly themes. If you have a picky eater, it may make it easier for them to know that not only were they consulted about the meals, they have something they like coming up soon. Possible themes are Mexican, Italian, American, crock pot night, leftover night and take-out night.

Getting meals on the table while everyone is running loose is indeed a challenge. I have five children, three of whom are usually doing homework during the dinner preparation hour. I try to have dinner put together before the kids come home from school. Setting the table is a different story though because that is where the homework typically gets done. By 5:30, homework time in the kitchen is completed so that I can get the table set. My two younger children don't have any homework so I let them play either in the basement or in their bedroom. I still have to keep an eye on them so that they don't get into mischief so setting the table usually takes more than the normal three minutes. I also enlist my older children's help once in a while with setting the table.

- Hildee W., Ohio

The Crock Pot — Your New Best Friend

Crock pots, though very retro, are still one of the most marvelous inventions known to at home moms (next to duct tape and locks on the bathroom doors). With one, you can cook a complete meal by simply tossing in the ingredients in the morning and forgetting about them for 6-8 hours. You can even make desserts (including cakes) using a slow cooker. If you have an older model that you received as a wedding present from your second cousin's Aunt Mildred, you may want to consider a newer model. They are much spiffier in the new millennium. Many of the new slow cookers have a removable pot, which makes for easier clean-up. If funds are tight, check your local thrift store, garage sales, or even eBay. There is always somebody out there who received two of them as wedding presents.

Even if you are intimidated by most cooking methods, cooking with a crock pot should make you feel like a pro. Instead of worrying about what's for dinner, just throw everything in after breakfast, enjoy the wonderful aromas all day long, then return to your kitchen around 6 with dinner ready to serve.

There are a few tips to keep in mind to make slow cooking a snap:

- Don't overfill it. When you are cooking with a crock pot, you want to leave enough space for everything to cook properly. If you have a large piece of meat (no laughing), you will need to cut it into smaller pieces.
- Put the veggies and potatoes on the bottom. Believe it or not, these actually cook slower than the meat.
- Taste it near the end of the cooking time. You will need to check to see how the flavor is. Keep salt, pepper and other basic seasonings like garlic salt handy.
- Don't add too much liquid at the beginning of the cooking time or you risk overflowing. Because the lid stays on during cooking, the liquid will not decrease — in fact, you will often end up with more juice.
- If you are adding pasta or rice, add it during the last 30 minutes of cooking time.
- Don't open the lid! Just like the oven, every time you open the lid, the temperature plummets. With the crock pot you add 20 - 30 minutes of cooking time to the meal. If you are a perpetual stirrer this will be a particularly difficult tip to follow.
- If "Low" is slow, "High" is quicker. Realize that if you start your meal late, you can increase the temperature to "High" to cut the cooking time in half.

All-In-One Meals, 30 Minute Meals & 6 Ingredients or Less

So many people have gotten away from cooking on a regular basis that there has been a big boom in methods to lure people back to cooking more frequently. Cooking shows have evolved from Julia Childs and Yan Can Cook, to the popular 30 Minute Meals and Quick Fix Meals, so obviously you and I are not the only ones with cooking issues. Check for show times on The Food Network or stop by their website for excellent recipes from past shows at www.foodnetwork.com.

The quick all-in-one meal is another way to get dinner on the table on a regular basis. All-in-one meals can be cooked in a crock pot, a skillet or baked in the oven. Forget about the dreaded onion and green bean casserole, there are a plethora of choices out there and cooking in one pot makes prep and clean up easier, which is ideal when dealing with the dinner hour chaos. Need recipes? Google the words "one pot meals".

The Bottom Line

Remember this — as long as it's edible you are making progress. Gourmet meals are all well and good, but when you are trying to prevent the kids from painting the dog, gourmet is the last thing on your mind. Cooking shouldn't cause you stress. Begin planning your meals and practice different cooking techniques to make your life easier.

After a while, you may find yourself actually enjoying cooking for your family. Ok, so this may be a stretch, but at least your family won't be bugging you about what's for dinner all the time, especially if you get good food on the table consistently.

Chapter 10:
Money, or Lack Thereof

When I contemplated going back to work, I met a childcare provider who let the kids in her care play with her vacuum cleaner. That was enough motivation for my husband and I to make me being at home work out, one way or another.

Money is one of the stickiest subjects for an at home mom. It's usually what causes the most fights and can give you more than your fair share of heartburn (yes, even more so than those bad days with the kids).

Since you are already staying at home, you obviously felt, for at least a short amount of time, that you would be able to make it on just one salary. Well, I can tell you this — 'feeling' like you can make it on one income is a lot different than the panicked reality you and your husband face around the third paycheck cycle after you start staying home. It is also a lot different than the feeling you get in the pit of your stomach when you realize that you are no longer getting a paycheck with your name on it.

Come to terms with this now. Chew on it, swallow it, digest it and move on. You no longer have an income. Nothing. Zip. Nada. Your entire financial situation now rests on your husband, who can't even remember to take out the garbage after being asked repeatedly for the past 5 years.

This is the harshest reality to face, but it has to be done. Better to process it now than to have it sneak up on you in the middle of the night. Now that I have you on the edge of panic, take a few deep breaths. Thousands and thousands of women have made staying at home work and so can you.

While the feeling of panic may never go away entirely, it does subside, especially on the days when you are home and you get to see your little pumpkin take their first steps or you get to volunteer in preschool for the first time.

Getting Over the Panic

It's hard not to wake up on occasion and wonder "What the hell was I thinking?" Here are some financial points to take comfort in:

1. You are no longer paying for childcare.
2. You are no longer paying for all the gas it takes to commute to and from work.
3. Your clothing expense will decrease (it's a lot cheaper to buy jeans than it was to buy suits and dry clean them regularly).
4. You will have fewer lunches out, since you won't be grabbing a bite to eat with co-workers on a regular basis (unless you enjoy taking the kids to McDonald's).

Unfortunately, these points don't always work when you wake up in the middle of the night crying because you feel like a money sucking leech for not working. To get through this feeling think about one of the following events that you would not get to experience if you were still working:

• Taking your child to their first day of school.
• Helping your child take their first steps.
• Sitting in a school assembly in the middle of the day.
• Volunteering at your child's school.

• Taking the kids out to lunch during the middle of the week.

• Waking up to your kid as an alarm clock and then cuddling in bed.

Are any of these events worth a paycheck? Not even close.

Saving Money

Despite the changes in your money flow, regardless of your husband's income, you will most likely still need to find ways to save money where you can. Becoming frugal can be a harrowing experience, especially if you were used to being able to buy what you wanted when you wanted.

Frugality is completely possible, but it is a learned process. Don't expect to become a pro at it overnight. There will be days when it is easy and hopefully those days will balance out the ones where you are almost in tears because you haven't bought yourself anything in months.

Kim Danger, of MommySavers.com, reminds SAHM's that "Frugality is a way of life. With any lifestyle change, it takes practice before it becomes habit. Make the commitment to change and after a few months it won't seem as tough. Realize that cutting back on material things doesn't have to affect your quality of life and in some ways can make it even more fulfilling."

Find ways to make changes in your lifestyle as early in your SAHM career as possible. The sooner you start, the sooner you can make it a habit. You will need to develop a thicker skin if it will bother you to not keep up with the Joneses — remember that you are doing this for your kids. The newer van or the trip to Mexico can wait. Your kids getting older will not.

25 Quick Ways to Save Money

1. Decrease your cable or satellite package. Do you really need access to Peruvian Mud Wrestling?

2. Eat dinner out less. You're learning to cook, remember?

3. Cook from scratch more (if you are capable of it). Food Network, Food Network, Food Network...

4. Buy less convenience foods. Instead of buying snack packs of crackers, buy the big box and put them in baggies.

5. Clip coupons for grocery shopping. Investing a single dollar in the Sunday paper can provide up to $50 in coupon savings.

6. Wash your own car instead of running it through the wash. Get the kids involved and turn it into a fun activity.

7. Develop a weekly meal plan to help curb spending at the grocery store. If you have a list and follow it, you are more likely to stay within your budget.

8. Rent movies instead of buying them. Try Netflix (www.netflix.com). For less than $10 a month, you can order movies online, they will be delivered in one day, and there is even a postage paid return envelope so all you have to do is drive by a mailbox when you're done with them. No late fees, no limits, no lines.

9. Check out movies from the library. Great option, especially for kid movies.

10. Form a babysitting co-op with friends. BIG savings plus quality time out with your husband.

11. Buy kids clothes at consignment stores. If you have not checked them out, you are missing the savings boat.

Especially good for special occasion clothes (for you too) that have only been worn once or twice!

12. Scour yard sales for good deals on necessities. Take a friend and make a fun day out of it.

13. Make birthday and holiday cards instead of buying them. They are more personal and each one you make saves between $2-$5!

14. Buy generic brands whenever possible. From medicine to macaroni, cheaper packaging + same main ingredients=BIG SAVINGS.

15. Since you are no longer commuting, many auto insurance companies offer lower rates for less driving. It's worth the call to find out.

16. If you have a larger family, buy your household supplies and food in bulk from a warehouse store. Go on weekends when samples are abundant and VOILA! – a free family meal!

17. When you go to kid activities, take your own snacks and drinks instead of buying them. This is always a healthier option anyway.

18. Decrease your cell phone package and make your calls during times when you get free calls.

19. If your cell phone offers free long distance, you can eliminate your long distance charges on your regular phone.

20. If you are a designer coffee junkie, find a brand of coffee at the grocery store that compares. Even if it is a few bucks more than the regular store brand coffee, it will still be cheaper than a Grande Mocha Latte at a coffee shop three times a week.

21. Resist the urge to buy your kids' clothes that you see just because they are 'cute.' I know this is a difficult one, but reducing these impulse buys can really add up and the kids will get over it (if they are even old enough to care in the first place).

22. Cancel your gym membership and work out at home. Go for a walk, run or bike ride with the kids instead.

23. Organize a toy swap with friends. This way all the kids have different toys to play with and no money is spent.

24. Start a small garden. If you have the room to do so, you can grow your own vegetables and have fresh produce at your disposal. Plus, the kids LOVE digging in the dirt.

25. Barter for goods. If you have a skill you can offer to people who have what you want, like handmade gifts during the holidays, offer your services in exchange for products.

Budget isn't a Four Letter Word

The only part that has given us trouble is the one thing that gives most people trouble. That would be making and sticking to a budget. With the movies that come out suddenly and the new books, great new homeschooling supplies, and gizmos for the home office that come out each day or week a budget can get very difficult to stick to unless you have a big stubborn streak that runs with your budget and not against it. Going over the budget once a week to adjust to sudden needs or new bills allows you to remind yourself of how you stand.

- Kathy E., Missouri

Setting a budget will help you save money and achieve your financial goals, despite how much you hate doing it. You no doubt took at least a peek at your budget before deciding to stay home. If you didn't, then you are a brave woman!

To set a budget, sit down with your husband and review the necessities. Include all different categories, like doctor visits and school supplies. Then look at the income you have to work with and figure out where it all needs to go. It's like cutting up a pie. If you have enough left over, you should always include a savings category for emergencies. This will prevent a surprise repair or emergency room visit from turning into a financial catastrophe. Even if it's an amount that you feel is trivial, every little bit saved helps.

To stick with the budget, track your spending on a weekly, and even daily, basis. Yes this is a pain in the butt to do, but if you know you have to account for it, it can actually help you curb spending. Keep a notebook in your purse or diaper bag or write it on your calendar every day. If certain expenses keep popping up (like, ahem, Starbucks or fast food) this will probably show you some areas that can be cut back or out completely.

A budget is an ongoing project and expect to revise it often, acknowledging that it will take a while for living on one income to become a regular habit. They say it takes three months of repeating the same behavior daily for it to become ingrained. It is worth the effort. If you have room for it, plan on a little discretionary money for you and your husband. If you have an amount that you can count on every month it will make the budgeting process less painful.

When you are out and you get bummed because you can't buy a new purse or a kickin' new shoes, just take a few minutes to reflect back on what it was like when you worked. Ah, yes, you remember the commutes in all that traffic, running late after being up with a sick kid all night, and dealing with a boss who smelled like stale coffee? You didn't really need those shoes, now did you?

Other Money Making Options

If there is still a small gap in your budget, there are several ways to fill it without returning to work full-time outside the home. Many employers, in an effort to retain quality woman employees, are finding ways for women to either work from home or work part-time. Even if your company doesn't already offer this, you may be able to convince them that your job could be done from home. Write up a professional, well fleshed out proposal for your boss. At the least, your boss will see that you are still interested in having some semblance of a career and may be willing to try and work something out.

If you have already severed ties with your company, finding a part-time job may be the answer to increased financial security. Depending on your husband's work hours, you may be able to find something to do in the evening and/or weekends when he is available to watch the kids. As an added bonus, he will be forced to take care of the kids on a regular basis and may develop an appreciation (or at least understanding) of what you do for the family, not to mention an increased closeness with his children.

If you decide you don't want to go this route, you can always join the thousands of women who own their own business. Many women think that owning a business has to be a tremendous time burden, but depending on your income needs, this may not be the case. See the chapter on working at home for more specific information.

Money and Husbands - Mr. Moneybags vs. Mommy the Leech

When I began staying home, one of the things that bugged me the most about money (other than having less of it) was the fact that I felt like I was a kid asking for their allowance whenever I approached my husband about money. I hated knowing that the money we had was earned by him and him alone. This was an issue I had to overcome (which was just one of many), but what I learned is that I was still contributing to the family; it just wasn't in monetary form. Even though you aren't working *outside* the home, you are still entitled to have access to the family money and your own discretionary money, if your budget allows. You are not a child. You are not worth less than your husband. You are still an equal partner. Any intimation otherwise needs to be nipped in the bud immediately.

Discuss how the family money will be handled. Will you do the bills or will he? How much money will be available for each spouse for their own personal use? Make sure you have a plan in place for how much each parent gets and when. You still need to be able to have a little bit of fun money for yourself, even if it is only enough to go to lunch with your friends once a month or a new book once in a while.

While you are having these discussions, you need to get a feel for your husband's thoughts about you being at home. Even if he has been enthusiastic about it since day one, there will invariably be a day when you are fighting about something related to the house and the subject of his income and your lack of one will come up. Be prepared. Don't automatically assume that he is resentful or that your life as a SAHM is doomed. Just know that it is ammunition in a marital fight and nothing more.

If it becomes more, if it becomes a painful barb that is constantly thrown in your face, you have a bigger problem that needs to be addressed immediately. Again, you should never be made to feel like you are subservient to your husband.

If money is causing resentment in your husband, get it out in the open. Make sure he understands how important it is to you to raise your kids. That it should be important to *both of you* – you should *both* feel like you are in it *together.* Maintaining an open dialogue is crucial for your marriage. If you both come to the decision that you need to go back to work, you will need to find quality, yet affordable childcare again. Make sure you take a close look at the costs, since they may have changed since you left the workforce and make the quality of the providers the highest priority. Remember, the money you end up spending on childcare may not be worth the little money you actually net. Chances are this process may convince your husband that you are doing the right thing by staying home and that the financial sacrifices are worth it. Again, these decisions need made together, as a *team* and as *equals.*

The Bottom Line

Money is a tough subject made even tougher when you go down to one income. Communicate with your husband about the different issues that come up. It may lead to some rough times so remember that the important thing is to stick together and have fun with the kids. Chances are they won't remember struggling here or there, but they will remember if you were unhappy about it.

SECTION 4
It's All About You!

Chapter 11:
Pack Your Bags, We're Going On a Guilt Trip

Chapter 12:
What About Me?

Chapter 13:
Surviving Bad Mommy Days

Chapter 14:
Stayin' Home and Making Money Anyway

Chapter 11:
Pack Your Bag, We're Going On a Guilt Trip

If there is one thing that acts as kryptonite to a mom, it's guilt. Not guilt over missing dinner at your in-laws' house or guilt at having too much dessert. It goes much deeper than that. This is the mind numbing, deep down to the bones type of guilt that we all experience at one time or another. It's Mommy Guilt.

Whether it's because you browsed a magazine for a few minutes instead of teaching your kids advanced math, because you don't have a house decorated like the ones in Better Homes and Gardens every holiday, or because you don't have the money to put your child in four extra curricular activities this school year, Mommy Guilt can be found lurking in the mental and emotional shadows. As an at home mom there is more time to allow this type of guilt to creep into our consciousnesses.

Moms seem to like to use guilt to keep themselves in check. It's like we are worried that without a healthy dose of it we would morph into impulse driven creatures that didn't care for our young. Relax. We're not built that way. Unless you have previously let loose and allowed your kids to eat off the floor or take the toaster into the bathtub, you will be fine without tripping over your own guilt all the time. Besides you need all your spare time for "tripping" over all those messes in the house.

Mommy Guilt comes in many different flavors, such as:

- Kid Guilt
- Money Guilt
- Work Guilt
- Home Guilt
- Feminism Guilt
- Personal Guilt

All of these forms of guilt are powerful and they will threaten to suck the life and confidence right out of you. The quicker you realize that it's counterproductive and vow to get over it, the better you will feel.

Kid Guilt

Kid guilt can spring up from anywhere. Let's say you are in the store with your children and it's been a rough morning. They are being loud, misbehaving, and touching everything. You get more than a little frustrated with said kids and firmly tell them to behave. Then, across the aisle, you spy a mom with more kids than you and they are behaving so well, she doesn't even have to raise her voice to them. Bam! There is a full blown case of kid guilt. You begin to wonder why *you* have to yell at your kids, why *you* couldn't be calmer, maybe *you're* a bad mom and on and on.

Don't do this to yourself. No matter what you see across the aisle, no one's children are perfect angels 24/7. Kids are kids and yours are going to have their bad days, just like you. Don't expect miracles just because you are with them more. If anything, this opens you up to more challenging days because they are so comfortable. The key to well behaved children lies not in mountains of guilt, but in your consistency with them. Rules, consequences and expectations, all laid out for them actually make a child secure and responsible, not unruly and belligerent. Not to mention consistency lays the groundwork for you to recapture a modicum of your AWOL sanity.

Home Guilt

How many times have you been even slightly embarrassed about the state of your house? How many times have you scolded yourself because your house "should" be clean because you are home all day? How many times have you pondered where, in fact, all those hours of the day have gone? SAHM's find it very difficult to not have something tangible to show for their long days. We all know how busy we are, but there never seems to be anything concrete to point to and say, "Look what I did today!"

Let it go! You are not home to be Molly Maid. You did not stay at home so you could clean baseboards and window sills. You are there to raise your kids, to interact with them, to be their touchstone. Dust will wait. Heck, if you leave it long enough, your kids can have fun drawing pictures and practicing their alphabet in it! Just enjoy being with them and let go of the unrealistic "House Beautiful" expectation.

Banish the image of June Cleaver from your head now. She was not real and even if she was, she never had to get arguing kids to school or pick up after a watermelon fight while she was keeping her house in pristine shape. *And* she wore pearls, heels and a dress! Get real! If I'm wearing pearls, heels and a dress it's because I'm playing dress up in my daughter's kitchen production of Cinderella! Remember, June was a TV character, not a real mom.

Money Guilt

This is a biggie for SAHM's. How dare we go out anywhere, at anytime, and spend any money when we aren't earning any ourselves? Ha! Remind yourself as often as necessary that what you are doing cannot be measured in monetary terms, because if it could, no one would be able to afford you. Have you priced 24 hour childcare recently? How about a live-in nanny? A personal chef?

Money guilt also stems from not being able to buy things

for the family on a whim. This is, perhaps, the biggest adjustment from two paychecks to one. In most two paycheck households, at least a portion of one covers the "fun things", the meals out, the movies, the new shoes, the video games. Being at home forces you to be more creative with your spending. Talk with your kids so they understand that while you may not be able to buy as much as before, you will have more family time. Kids are very intuitive and, quite frankly, when they grow up, they will remember if they were loved unconditionally, not the number of Nintendo games you bought them.

We are tight and do without a lot of extras. I feel a little guilty when my kids want something, or when they are interested in a class or league that is out of our budget.

I just remind myself that I am doing the best thing for my kids, and that family is a lot more important than money, possessions or status.

-Tina S., CA

Work Guilt

When you worked, you felt guilty because you were *at* work. Now that you *don't* work, you feel guilty for that. Maybe you feel like a slacker for not having a job or that you are wasting your education or that you are wasting all the time you spent working your way up the corporate ladder.

Nothing could be further from the truth. You are not suddenly less of a person for staying home; you are, in fact, more.

First of all, you are not wasting your education by staying home. And you did not leave your brain cells or degree behind when you collected your last paycheck. They're all still there. As an at home mom, your children will reap the benefits of your knowledge and will grow up understanding the value of education. Remain confident in yourself as a thinking, educated adult. Besides, don't you want to have the ability to articulate your thoughts without using terminology from Blues Clues?

You may also worry about losing your footing in the workplace, especially if you worked for years to climb the corporate ladder before deciding to stay home. It's a valid concern, but work *will* always be there in some form or another. Once your kids are grown, you will probably have at least 20 years to look forward to working again. Concentrate on preventing your brain from turning to mush and vow to keep up in your field, maybe even enroll in an online course or two, and you will have little difficulty reentering the work force.

Feminism Guilt

If you are even the slightest bit feminist, it may bother you that you are, in some people's eyes anyway, throwing away the last 60 years of the women's movement to end up right where woman were back in the 1950s.

Roll this guilt up in your least favorite bra and burn it. It's simply not true.

Women today have choices and with the rise in work-at-home businesses, many moms are choosing to forego the rat race to do what matters most to them. Raising your kids does not mean that you are killing the message of feminism; it simply means you are making different choice. And ultimately that is what the feminist movement is really all about — having CHOICES.

Personal Guilt

As moms, we tend to rival Joan of Arc as world class martyrs. We make sure we do anything and everything that needs to be done for the kids, the husband and the house at the drop of a hat. Taking time for ourselves, *doing* something for ourselves, simply never seems to make the priority list. In order to do it all and be it all for everyone else, we don't just put our own needs on the back burner, we tend to push them clear off the stove.

Being an at home mom does not make you less of a person, in fact it makes you more of one. After all, what is more *personal* than raising intelligent, responsible, nurtured human beings? In that same vein, your SAHM status does not decrease your need, *your right*, to have something outside of motherhood. What you are doing is a job. Sure, it is a labor of love compared to balancing accounts or selling items in the outside work world, but it *is* a job with real demands, emotional ties, time commitments and stresses. And everyone who works needs some time to recharge their batteries. If you don't, you are just setting yourself up for major adjustment, identity and resentment issues down the road.

Let your family (read - husband) know that it is imperative that you get time to yourself and that locking yourself in the bathroom while the kids are screaming at you does not count. You deserve to be a well rounded individual with interests you pursue outside your family. You will be a better wife and mother and when Mommy is happy, *everyone* is happy.

You must value yourself as an individual and maintain your own identity outside being a Mommy and Wife. Sure, in your day to day life, you are, for the most part, *functional*, but you deserve time to simply be *fun* too. Remember, as an at home mom you are not a slave to your family. And if anyone begins to treat you that way do something about it — quick!

The Bottom Line

Despite the fact that you no longer have a full time J.O.B., you are still a valuable person. Accept that there will be times when some form of Mommy Guilt will creep up on you and you will find yourself lamenting some perceived shortcoming in your performance. That's normal. Just don't let it permeate your life or settle in to stay. Give yourself a few minutes to wallow in sorrow, frustration, even resentment and then move on. You are not less of a mom, wife or woman because you want to be at home with your kids. You are making a choice that will positively impact everyone around you for the rest of their and YOUR lives.

If other people are the cause of your guilt, concentrate on removing them from your life or simply ignoring them. You may not be able to change their minds or point of view towards you being at home, but you *can* be secure in your own feelings about your choice, which is all that matters anyway. Seek your own approval — not someone else's. Everyone has their opinions about what a mom should and should not be like, and amazingly, the most vocal ones are typically the ones without any children or frame of reference for what they are saying. Ignore them.

Just don't let it get to you. If you have to, come up with a snarky response that can roll off your tongue at a second's provocation. My personal favorite? "The world is so much bigger than I thought when I was working. How sad for you that yours is still so one dimensional."

Chapter 12:
What About Me?

Taking regular time out for yourself is vital to your survival as a SAHM. We have all heard the cliché "If Momma ain't happy, ain't nobody happy", but this is so much more true when you are around the kids all the time. Many SAHM's feel so guilty for having *any* feelings of discontent or frustration that they worsen their situations by *never* taking any time for themselves at all. Unfortunately all this is going to do is leave you emotionally drained and seething with resentment. Trust me, the kids will drain you enough — why add to it?

Part of being a SAHM is acknowledging, without any guilt, that as with any job, you are not going to feel completely fulfilled 24 hours a day. No one likes their job *all the time*. There are ups and downs, highs and lows, good times and bad times, strike outs and homeruns. Feeling a little trapped every now and then is perfectly fine too. It does not mean you are a bad mother, far from it. The love you feel for your children is not what wavers. Rather, it's the simple weariness of doing the same thing day in and day out for years and years that sends these waves through your emotional ocean. Accept them, accept that you are human, and you will not drown in a sea of guilt.

Getting time to yourself is like getting regular maintenance on your vehicle. We know we need to do it, but we don't always take the time to get it done. And what happens? Left without attendance for too long, the engine breaks down. You are no different. You need your emotional oil changed on a regular basis, you deserve to get detailed for a special night out and you definitely need your battery jumped from time to time.

There are many ways to make sure you get time for yourself. The easiest way is to set up a system with your husband that guarantees you some "me" time daily. It can be as little as 15 minutes (though obviously more is better), but it is *your* time. With it you can read, take a bubble bath or just sit in a quiet room without someone yelling your name every 10 seconds. Use these time outs to re-center yourself, breathe deeply and emerge with a smile.

Reasons to take time for yourself on a regular basis:
Time outs will prevent burn outs

Remember when you were working and there was always talk about burnout? "Make sure you don't work too hard, or you'll burn out." and "Don't only focus on your work or you'll burn out." If burnout was a danger when you could leave your job at the end of the day, how much more prone is a SAHM who cannot escape her job at all? Listen, you can love your kids more than life itself, but if you don't prioritize time outs away from them, you will begin to crisp around the edges and eventually suffer a total emotional flambe'. You might begin feeling bored or you may notice that you lose your temper easier than before. These are the first smoke signals of burnout — and in this case, where there's smoke, there is definitely fire.

It will remind you that you are a separate person

You obviously like being a mom — if you didn't you wouldn't have decided to be at home. Nevertheless, you are also *you*. A separate, thinking, interesting person. And if you are always doing things for your family and always giving emotionally to your kids and husband, you can begin to lose sight of who you are without them. Maintaining a separate identity, one that goes by your first name, not a title like Mommy or Wife, is integral to your continued growth and happiness as a full person. You had interests outside of the little rugrats who are currently running your house — continue to pursue them (the interests, not the rugrats).

Every time you begin to do something for yourself and you feel that guilt creeping over you like a dark shadow, remind yourself that it will make you a better mom and wife, and that everyone will benefit.

Schedule it to make it happen

To really get in the habit of taking time for yourself, set a regular day to do your chosen activity. Treat it just like you would a doctor's appointment, because it's just as important to your health. You could:

- Have dinner with your girlfriends — Enjoy ordering food that does not automatically come with french fries and crayons.
- Declare a movie night with a friend — How long has it been since you saw a movie *not* produced by the mouse with the big round ears anyway?
- Go get a pedicure, manicure or other pampering type "stuff" — These all require you to sit still which is pure bliss for a SAHM.
- Take a class at your local community college or parks and recreation department — You will challenge yourself and make new friends in the process.
- Get a massage — if you have a massage school nearby, they

often offer discounts for letting a student give the massage — Nothing takes the edge off like a delicious shoulder and neck massage.

Find a hobby

A hobby is the perfect reason to make time for you. Now that you don't have to worry about sick days, missed school programs and weekend parenting, take some time to focus on something you want to do for a change.

If you don't have a hobby, explore all the options until you find one that clicks with you. Scrapbooking, painting, cake making, knitting, dancing – they can be a great way to make new friends and provides a focus outside of motherhood. There are many places you can learn and practice a new hobby. Look for classes offered through your local parks and recreation departments or check out the introductory level classes of your local community college for ideas.

Here are some hobby ideas that might pique your interest:

• Scrapbooking
• Photography
• Knitting
• Needlepoint
• Writing
• Painting
• Play an instrument

Whatever you choose, make sure it is something you can do away from your family at least part of the time. Remember, the idea is to get some time *away* from them so you can appreciate them, and they you, *more* when you return. Heavy emphasis on the latter as they will get an idea of just how the house runs (or doesn't run) without you.

Create a "Mommy Network"

As moms, we are always talking to other people about our kids, making sure that the situations we are going through, and our reactions to them, are, in fact, normal. Use your kids and their activities to create your own Mommy Network. This group of women can be your light at the end of the tunnel on the bad days. After all, who better to understand and empathize than those living your same life? When I left teaching, several of my teaching friends left the following year upon having kids. We now get together once a month and talk about life at home and how we are getting along with our children. It's now one of my favorite days of the month and something I completely look forward to. The kids are still there, of course, but this is as much a play date for me as for them.

In the home — Mommy Time Outs

On the days when your oldest child gets in trouble at school and your toddler is trying to duct tape your cat to the wall, it's time to take a Mommy Time Out. This is when you to remove yourself from a stressful situation and recharge your batteries by engaging in an activity *just for you* for a minimum of 15-30 minutes. I began doing this with my husband and now even my oldest will tell me when I need my own time out.

The number one Mommy Time Out rule is that you cannot clean and you cannot do something that would be considered a chore. So, if you like doing home improvement projects, building

something might be fun. For me, this would be more like a pun-
ishment, so I wouldn't choose this activity during my time out,
but to each her own.

Another rule is that you must be allowed to have your time
out without any interruption or interference. If you are reading a
book and the kids are banging on the door, explain to your husband that the time starts over for you just like it does when kids
are in time out. After a few restarts of a 15 minute time out that
turns it into an hour long one, he will probably get the idea. If he
doesn't, inform him that he needs to do this for you so you don't
end up on the evening news in a feature story about "moms who
have lost it". Make sure you don't laugh when you say this, so he
can't tell whether you are kidding or not.

Here are some different activities you can do around the
house for your Mommy Time Out:
• Read a chapter of a book
• Look at a magazine
• Write in a journal
• Organize your pictures
• Scrapbook
• Take a bubble bath
• Work in your garden
• Go for a walk
• Take a power nap
• Paint your nails
• Email friends
• Light some candles and listen to your favorite music

Change Your Routine

When things begin to get stale or feel like they aren't working for you at the moment, switch things up. The same way kids get bored doing the identical things day in and day out, you need to make sure you are keeping things interesting for yourself too. Even if it is as simple as rotating laundry days, play dates, shopping days, or the stores you shop in each week, it will keep things fresh. This is the key to defeating burn out.

The Bottom Line

Make sure that you are still doing things for yourself on a regular basis. Prioritize YOU. On the really tough days, you may need some slightly more serious intervention, whether it's just chatting with a friend or going to the grocery store by yourself. You need to make sure you remain your own person.

Chapter 13:
Bad Mommy Days

I no longer have little ones at home, but I remember times when I didn't handle things very well. One day the phone rang and my three-year-old answered. It was my mother.

"Can I speak to your Mom?" she asked.

"No," answered the little guy emphatically.

"Why not?" asked my mother.

Pause. "She's in her room pounding on the wall and screaming."

I was.

-Lynn C., Washington

We all have our bad days, but bad days as an at home momma are particularly acute because we can't go hide from them. In the work world we could walk to a different area of the building, go to the bathroom, vent to a coworker, shut a door for a few moments, or watch the clock till the end of the day. Now, as a SAHM, there is no respite, there are no doors to close — a closed door is an invitation for disaster — and no matter where you go in the house, the kids will follow like they are loving little puppies and you are wearing beef jerky underwear.

There are generally two different types of Bad Mommy Days — those that are kid induced and those that are mommy induced. The key to not letting these eat you alive is having a strategy to get through them. And trust me, when you have a particularly tough day, the ultimate goal is simple: survival.

Kid Induced Bad Mommy Days

These days are tough to handle and like a thunderstorm,

you can feel them coming on. The clouds typically begin to gather when a child is teething, suffering from a series of bad dreams, or crying because the tag on their shirt is rubbing them the wrong way. The effects are cumulative, often beginning before daylight when said child wakes you from a delicious dream starring you and Denzel Washington, Brad Pitt or Antonio Banderas. This obviously does not start the day on a high note and your mood rapidly rolls downhill from here.

The techniques to get through days like this are sometimes drastic, but remember the goal is to get away from counting the hours, minutes and seconds until your husband gets home and to maintain as much peace and sanity as humanly possible. Note of caution: In a nod to Murphy's Law, *really* bad days usually coincide with the days your husband has to work late or when he gets stuck in a traffic jam on the way home.

The key to getting through Bad Mommy Days is to throw your kids off their game. Their whining, complaining and grousing are predictable — in fact, that's why you are in this mood to begin with — so you will need to do something out of the ordinary and different from the normal routine. Make milk shakes for lunch. Build a sheet fort in the living room. Run around the backyard as fast as you all can. Not only will everyone end up with smiles on their faces — you included (after all, who doesn't like a drinking a good milk shake in a sheet fort after running through the backyard like a mad woman?) — but unexpected activities like this usually help jolt kids out of a funk.

It will take you roughly 200% more effort to get through these days without snapping, so try to be extra loving. You are aware of what you are feeling and you are the only one who can keep it under control. Your children should never be your sounding board or the target of your bad mood. Besides, while you may need something a bit stronger (like that end of day glass of Merlot), sometimes kids just need extra "Momma Lovin" to get through their day.

Survival Ideas Around The House

• Pull out the craft supplies - Pull out the craft supplies and let them go to town. A mess made with glitter or cotton balls is a much better alternative to a screaming kid.

• Throw on a movie - Every kid should have a movie that they can veg out to. Whether it is a Baby Einstein or Disney video makes no difference. As long as it gets and keeps their attention, it'll soothe and calm them enough to either fall asleep or at least stop being so grating.

• Just add water - Kids love water. Let them play with a spray bottle or give them a mid day bath. If you play with them in the bathroom, watch them around the toilet. My son once put an entire roll of toilet paper in the toilet during the two minutes of privacy I gave him while potty training.

• Magazine Scavenger Hunt - Give them a few old magazines and have them look for certain items or words. If you want to really get fancy and have several kids involved, you could make a list of words for each child and award a silly prize to the one who finds all their words first. (Prizes can be as funny as the winner being addressed as "King Monkey" the rest of the day.) Be careful when you pass out the magazines — as I mentioned in an earlier chapter, you don't want little Johnny leafing through Glamour and cutting out pictures of bras and thongs, now do you?

- Put on Music and Get Funky - Turn on the radio and dance! If your kids just stand and look at you, dance even crazier. Eventually they will crack a smile and join in the fun. To switch it up, put on oldie music or something out of the ordinary like reggae.
- Do the same thing, but with a twist - If they like to color, give them colored pencils or some of your pens or pencils to use. If they don't want to get dressed, make it "Backwards Day" and make them wear everything backwards.

Make it a Special Day

To really throw them off their game, take kids somewhere special. Besides the usual stand-ins of McDonald's and Burger King, you can also go walk around the mall, go to the museum or local park or plan a hike through your own neighborhood. The idea is to change the scenery for all of you, grab some fresh air and recharge your batteries. Special Note — If you have a toddler, don't even worry about being creative, just hit Mickey D's. You never know when Toddler Vesuvius is going to erupt and at least in a McDonald's, no one will even blink.

Kids are always enamored with the mere idea of a special day. So declare a household holiday. Annual Backwards Day! Upside Down Day! Inside out Day! Popcorn Day! Any silly idea you can think of will find the kids having so much fun trying to find ways to follow the day's theme that they will forget they were ever even having a bad day.

Out of the Ordinary

Have some special items on hand to divert their attention. These can include:

- Window Crayons - These wipe off easily, so let kids make a mural on the sliding glass door or other window.
- Bathtub Crayons - Let them color in the bathtub. These crayons are designed to wash off easily, so they can paint themselves the color of the rainbow then you can shower it off.
- Finger Paint - Pull out some butcher paper or paper bags and let them go to work.
- Flour Pictures - Pour some flour on a cookie sheet and let them create pictures.

Remember: Sometimes making a mess is worth the trade off in terms of peace, happy children and your sanity.

Mom Induced Bad Mommy Days

These are the days I dread the most. These are the ones that we create. The kids haven't necessarily done anything wrong, yet we are moody, irritable, snippy and our mouths tend to be loaded like double barrel shotguns. These days can be caused by many different factors, including PMS, illness, financial issues and every woman's favorite — having a fight with the husband. None of these are your children's fault, so you need to mitigate your nasty temper and simmering emotions as much as possible.

On these days, you will need to direct extra effort towards not letting the kids add to your emotional crock pot, making it boil over. Unfortunately, at least in my house, these are the days when one of the kids will try to wash themselves with their broc-coli and applesauce or dump out the entire toy box and start a game of hockey.

The best strategy to have in place for days like this is the

Quiet Time Out. This should be a component of every day anyway — children need to learn how to calm down, be quiet, be comfortable with themselves, and enjoy a book for 20 minutes or so. Quiet Time Outs will be life savers on days when your PMS is coursing buckshot through your veins, your husband is on your "list", the toilet has overflowed, the dog has poopy butt, and you just burned the second batch of cookies in a row. Your patience will be pushed to the absolute limits, so you may require more drastic measures, although probably not as drastic as two o'clock martinis. Keep a hidden stash of chocolate and wait to mix the drinks till Daddy comes home.

Saving Your Sanity Ideas

• Put on a movie for the kids. Find one that will keep the kid's attention and do one of the following:

• Call a girlfriend — This is a perfect time to rely on someone in your support network. Call someone who will listen to you complain and sympathize with you. Sometimes venting is all you need to feel better.

• Look at a magazine or read a chapter of a book. Again, doing something for YOU will help regain your emotional balance.

• Do a few scrapbook pages. Creative outlets are great stress relievers.

• Paint your toenails. Feeling feminine and pretty is an amazing ego boost.

Whatever you choose, make sure it is something you consider pampering. Margaritas are only considered pampering when you have another adult to share them with. Save them for

Girls' Night Out, otherwise you will look like one of those tipsy stay at home moms constantly parodied in movies from the 80s.

You cannot completely prevent the bad days — you are human, plus you have estrogen. But being cognizant of their onset and symptoms will help you cope with and limit their effects on your household. Diffuse potential blow ups by making sure you are getting/taking enough time for yourself.

The Bottom Line

Bad days as an at home mom stink because there is usually no where to hide from them. Ensure you develop some strategies identifying and dealing with days like this so you aren't as tempted to become a runaway. Whether it's because of the kids or because of PMS, having some innovative ideas and systems to survive will keep everyone from becoming your verbal victims. Just don't let Mommy Guilt get to you for letting the kids watch movies or for taking them somewhere special. It's not going to spoil them, kill them or turn them into psychopaths. Remember — the key is survival.

Chapter 14:
Stayin' Home and Making Money Anyway

Working from home is a lot like cooking a Thanksgiving dinner. You know that it's a lot of work, but you do it anyway because the results are so darned good. Not everyone can work from home successfully — it takes a lot of effort to be able to strike the right balance between work and family when you are around both all the time. However, if you can juggle the balls successfully, you may never go back to working outside the home again.

Why Bother?

If you are right on the cusp of being able to afford to stay home, working from home may be the answer you are looking for. Even a small income may be all it takes to allow it to happen.

If you are used to being a working mom and miss the mental stimulation of a job, working from home can be the key to your sanity and happiness. It will give you a focus outside of being a mom and allow you to make some spending money while giving you an excuse for utilizing higher brain functions.

Choosing a Business

Choosing a business is like choosing new shoes. If you rush into the store and grab the first pair you see, you may end up with an uncomfortable fit. However, when you take your time, walk around the department with them on, admire them in the mirror, and imagine them with your favorite outfit, you know the shoes will fit and you will feel comfortable and excited with your purchase.

There are a plethora of options out there for a mom who wants to work from home. The most obvious choice is to start your own business in a field related to your former profession. If you were a marketing director for a company, you could set up shop as a marketing consultant for new businesses, as a copywriter, or create a PR firm for a specific type of business. If you were a teacher, you could become a tutor (tutoring high school students facing their SATs averages about $35 an hour), start an after school homework club from your house, or become a homeschooling consultant. If you were a waitress or house cleaner, run away now because staying home won't be very different from what you are used to.

Liz Folger, author of Making Money From Home and owner of BizyMoms.com, suggests that moms "look at your hobbies, and interests. What do you already enjoy doing? Sometimes we overlook the things that come easy to us and think they come easy to everybody else. But it doesn't work that way. We are all born with special talents and interests. You can use these to make money from home. When looking for a business to start, is there a way you can use the current skills in your job in your future home business? Or maybe you want to use your creative side and are unable to do that in your current job. Follow your dreams, believe in what you have to offer."

If you were in a profession that you want to get away from or you want to do something a little more low key, you could consider joining a direct sales company. With this type of business you are usually free to run things the way you see fit and you keep a percentage of the sales of all your products. There are direct sales companies for a number of products, including:

Makeup

Jewelry

Scrapbooking supplies

Mini Greeting Cakes

Adult Products

Cooking Supplies

Legal Services

Food

Coffee

Spa Products

Greeting Cards

Kids toys

Cleaning Products

Health Products, including vitamins

Books

Clothes

Purses

Wine

Pet Products

Choosing a Direct Sales Company

If you decide to join a direct sales company, do plenty of research first. There are hundreds of scams disguised as direct sales, so do your homework, check out backgrounds, Better Business Bureau reports, etc, to prevent becoming an "It Happened To Me" story. You need to identify an area/company that you like and would be happy to be immersed in. If you aren't into their products and don't use them on a daily basis, it will probably be more difficult for you to sell them.

Here are some questions to ask about the company:

1. How long has it been in business?

2. How much is the sign up fee?

3. Are you required to carry inventory?

> Even if you are told that you can succeed without having an inventory, know that it will be much more difficult to succeed without one.

4. How is commission figured out?

5. What is the commission percentage?

6. Is there a way for you to set up shop on the internet?

> Many companies will either allow you to pay a monthly fee for a 'company' website or will allow you to sell their products on your own site.

7. What are the sales quotas? Are they monthly, quarterly, yearly?

8. What type of advertising is acceptable by the company?

9. What type of support do they offer new and continuing members?

10. How many reps are there in your area?

11. How many other direct sales companies are in this market? If there are more than a couple, the market may be saturated and it will be more difficult to make money.

Points for Success

Whether you start from scratch or join a direct sales company, there are a few factors to keep in mind.

• Interest Level - Make sure you are choosing something in which you have a high level of interest. To make money with it, you will have to engross yourself in whatever field you choose. If you aren't that into it in the first place, success will be virtually impossible to achieve.

• Niche - Once you have a basic idea, see if you can narrow it further. The more specific your niche is, the less competition you will have. Just make sure your niche isn't so narrow that your customer base is miniscule. Organic Earthworm Pasta probably has a very limited market.

• Income Requirements - Decide what type of income you need/want to make per month. Is this a realistic goal with the business you have chosen?

• Time to Invest - Think about how much time you will have to invest to make a profit. Remember, the idea of working from home is finding the balance between family and job.

• Work Schedule - Set a realistic work schedule and stick to it. Can you work while the baby naps or during preschool or would you prefer to work in the evenings? Once you decide on a schedule, stick to it just as you did when you worked outside the home.

Setting Up Shop

Once you decide what business you wish to pursue, you need to get ready to launch.

• Contact your local government to determine if you need a business license.

• Set up a separate bank account for your business. You don't necessarily need a business checking account — you will save money on monthly fees initially by setting up another personal account.

• Make sure you have marketing materials, including business cards, flyers and brochures.

• Set up a website. Even if you don't know HTML, you can set up a website using an online service or a web template. Hosting will run anywhere between $3 -$10 per month, but is worth it. In this day and age, people expect everything to have *.com* attached to it.

- Write out a plan. It doesn't have to be a formal business plan, but you need to give some thought to where you want your business to go and how you will get it there. Include a short description of your business, a mission statement, a basic marketing plan of attack, estimates of your start up costs and projected income.

- Get your name out there. If you offer a service, offer to perform it for free in exchange for use in your portfolio and a testimonial. If you can't do that, offer a discount to those who help you get started.

For more startup information, check the resource section at the back of the book.

Funding Your Startup

Since money will probably be a bit tighter as you switch to one income, look for other ways to fund your business startup. You could:

- Have a garage sale.
- Sell items on eBay.
- Use the profit from your first sales to fund your start up fees.
- Take out minimal funds from a retirement account.
- Ask family members for a small loan.
- Barter with a business who offers what you need (for example — accountant, web designer, etc.)
- Take minimal equity out of your home.

Folger advises moms not go crazy spending money on advertising. "We think we need to spend all this money on ads and that can get so costly. A person needs to see an ad about 6 or 7 times before they think about buying. This can really cost you some money, money you don't have. Think about all the FREE ways you can advertise. Press releases, telling all your family and friends what you're up to, getting on your local talk radio and talking about your business, giving presentations at local clubs in your area, giving your product or service away at charity auctions. Think free, free, free."

Managing Your Time

Once you get your business up and running, you need to determine what procedures are required to run it smoothly and decide how you will complete these procedures. For example, if your goal is to perform one marketing task per week, you need to develop a strategy and schedule to make it happen.

Managing your time is also important to prevent your business from invading and taking over your home life. It can be really difficult to turn off the business side of your brain when you are around your workplace (i.e. home) all the time. Resist the temptation to work all the time. We already have enough built in guilt simply by being moms, so don't add to it by feeling like you are neglecting your kids in order to make your business successful. If you begin feeling this way, chances are there is a good reason. Yes, home businesses require a certain amount of sacrifice, but you shouldn't make your family one of them.

Work on creating a balance between working enough to make your business successful and having the mental and physical energy to still be a good mom. And if you figure out the secret to this one, please let me in on it!

Here are a few tips to help you manage your time better.

1. Set a Schedule. Define your work hours then stick to them as much as possible.

2. Create to do lists. You may not get everything on them complete, but it will clear your mind to have them on paper.

3. Assign task priorities. Take a look at what you need to accomplish and then determine how important is each task. You may really enjoy doing 'research' online, but if you need to get a proposal together for a potential client, this should come first.

4. Stay Organized. Keep everything relatively cleaned up so you can find what you need when you need it. After a few times searching frantically for work papers that have somehow become mixed in with your kid's homework, you'll get the idea.

Working Around the Kids

As with any child, my son wants my attention constantly throughout the day. I have set up his own "work station" next to mine where we can work on the computer together. He also tests my children's products, telling which are a hit and which need more development. (For instance, I was attempting to make organic bears, but the first one my son saw, he said he loved the RAT. He was correct and it did greatly resemble a rodent rather than the bear I was aiming for. I've set that project back for future redesign.) My son also helps put things together, mail boxes and organize.

- Camille F., Virginia

Working at home around the family takes skill, patience and oh yeah, more patience. If you can find a way to get your kids involved, they will be a lot less resentful when you are working because they know that they can be included too. Kids can help with mailing, organizing supplies, licking stamps and envelopes and even filing if they are old enough. You can also make a kid office, complete with their own office supplies and even an old non-working computer keyboard. Then they can work along side you.

If this doesn't work, you have a few options left. The best one is to work while they are napping, in school or after they head to bed. This will give you the peace and quiet you need in order to concentrate on business tasks. If this doesn't work or you need to squeak more time out for a big project, you can work while the kids are playing. If you have a laptop, then you can type away while they play in the same room. You can also work the old fashioned way with a pen and paper. If you have orders to process or put together, this can be done on the kitchen table while the kids eat snack.

Another way to get more done with kids around is to make good use of all your available time. Think about all the time that is wasted while waiting at the doctor's office, while waiting for sports practice to end, waiting for after school pick up and even stop lights. Keep some work with you wherever you go and you can work in these extra chunks of time. If you do this consistently, think about how much extra time you can come up with. If you have trouble focusing in your small bursts of time, you can still make lists, brainstorm marketing idea and even outline your weekly goals. The key is to work on being as productive as you can in the time that you have.

Being Successful

Running a successful business takes time and effort. Unless you are in direct sales (and even then) don't expect to make a significant chunk of change for a while. People need to get used to seeing your name out there. This proves that you have enough longevity to survive in the business world. You also need to:

1. Take yourself seriously.

If you don't take yourself and your business seriously, why should anyone else? When you go to make a business decision ask yourself "Would Bill Gates or the CEO of Pepsi do this?" Of course you aren't that big, but treating your business like it is that size will send the right impression to your customers.

This means you have to make a name for yourself with follow through, follow up, and on time job completion. Give more than they expect and maintain the highest standards.

2. Present a professional image.

Even though you work at home around your kids, it is not kosher to have your kids screaming in the background while you are taking a sales call. Keep the same level of professionalism that you had when you worked outside your home. Only talk to clients when you are able to do so without the fear of one of your children announcing their potty training success or demanding Goldfish crackers in the background.

Be professional with all of your client contact, including email. There is a reason your email program has a spell checker. Use it. Would you take a company seriously who WROTE

YOU A MESAGE LIKE THIS? Didn't think so. Working from home is no excuse for not using business common sense, good grammar and full punctuation. And never, never, never, include emoticons in a business email. No :O) or :-/

3. Be Flexible.

Being a SAHM is not a cakewalk and working from home simply places an additional layer on top. There will be days when you get sick or one of your kids is under the weather or your dog barfs on important work papers or your kids won't take a nap so you can make an important call. Sometimes this all happens on the same day. Relax. When you work from home there are many different dynamics simultaneously at play. Be willing to go with the flow and just do what you can to stay on top of things while keeping your sanity relatively intact.

4. Keep your head up.

Being successful at a business takes a long time and a lot of effort. Don't become discouraged when overnight success doesn't materialize. At the very least, you are setting a good example for your kids by showing them that you can, a) do something other than clean up after them, and b) work hard at something for an extended period of time.

The Bottom Line

If you choose to work from home, keep this one thing in mind. You are doing this to make your stay at home choice more financially comfortable. If you start dreaming about how much better work was when you worked outside the home, it's time to reevaluate the choices you have made.

You know the corny saying "Do what you love and the money will follow"? It may often seem like the money is way behind you, but it will eventually catch up with you as long as you keep your head up and follow the correct path.

Resources

Obviously, internet resources for stay at home moms are changing all the time. The following web resources were current at the
time of this book's printing – for more resources and current
links, visit my site www.AlanaMorales.com and click on
Domestically Challenged: Links.

If you have a resource you want to share that isn't listed, please
email me at Links@AlanaMorales.com. Enjoy!

General Stay At Home Mom Links

Mothers and More
www.mothersandmore.org

4 Moms At Home
www.4momsathome.com

Mocha Moms – An organization for at home moms of color.
www.mochamoms.org

About.com's At Home Parents Site
www.homeparents.about.com

Aiming At Moms
www.aimingatmoms.com

Family And Home Network
www.familyandhome.org/index.php

ClubMom

www.clubmom.com

Craft & Coloring Resources

DLTK's Printable Crafts for Kids

www.dltk-kids.com

Printable crafts, coloring sheets, cards, and other projects.

Enchanted Learning

www.enchantedlearning.com

Educationally based crafts and activities.

Everything Preschool

www.everythingpreschool.com

Preschool themes and activities.

Amazing Incredible Handwriting Worksheet Maker

www.handwritingworksheets.com

A great site if you want to print out a customized letter tracing sheet.

Primary Games

www.primarygames.com

Crafts, coloring sheets, puzzles, and basic learning materials.

Coloring Book Fun

www.primarygames.com

Coloring sheet site with a lot of commercial characters and a lot of ads.

Papa Jan

www.papajan.com

Click on the activity pad for preschool activities, connect the dots and cutting practice.

Family Fun

www.familyfun.com

Official site for the magazine.

Free Kid Crafts

www.freekidcrafts.com

Crafts for toddlers and preschoolers.

Making Friends

www.makingfriends.com

Lots of great printables, plus easy, cheap crafts to buy.

Child Fun Family Website

www.childfun.com

Lots of coloring sheets and crafts, but it also has a lot of ads.

Creativity Portal

www.creativity-portal.com

Click on Kids Crafts, lots of ads.

Free Printables

www.free-printables.com

Lots of great crafts, very commercial site.

Character Websites (with games, crafts and coloring sheets)

Nick Jr.

www.nickjr.com

Includes Blue's Clues and Dora the Explorer.

Playhouse Disney on Disney Online

www.playhousedisney.com

Includes Little Einsteins, Higgley Town Heroes and JoJo's Circus.

PBS Kids

www.pbskids.com

Includes Clifford, Arthur, or Dragon Tales among many, many others.

Sesame Street

www.sesameworkshop.com

Has all of your favorite Sesame Street characters, including Elmo.

Discovery Kids

http://kids.discovery.com

Getting Out Resources

National Parks and Recreation Association

http://www.nrpa.org/content/default.aspx?documentId=497

I know this is a long link, but it will take you to a directory of all of the state parks and recreation departments.

Parenthood

www.parenthood.com

This is the main site for many local parenting magazines. Click on local links to see if there is a link for your city.

Playgroup Resources

Matching Moms

www.matchingmoms.org

Mothers of Preschoolers

www.mops.org

Moms Offering Moms Support (MOMS)

www.momsclub.org

My Playgroups

www.myplaygroups.com

SAHM Meetup Groups

www.sahm.meetup.com

Online Communities for Moms Resources

Babycenter

www.babycenter.com

IVillage

www.ivillage.com

Yahoo! Groups

www.Yahoo.com

Google Groups

www.Google.com

MSN Groups
www.groups.msn.com

SheKnows
www.talk.sheknows.com

My Momma Said
www.mymommasaid.com

Cleaning Resources
FlyLady
www.flylady.com

Organize Tips
www.organizetips.com

Organized Mom
www.organized-mom.com

Organized Home
www.organizedhome.com/index.html

Calendar/Planner Resources
Franklin Covey
www.franklincovey.com

Go Mom planner
www.gomominc.com

The Busy Woman's Daily Planner
www.thebusywoman.com

The Family Planner
www.thefamilyplanner.com

Chaos Companion
www.mommyhulabaloo.com

Cooking Resources
General Cooking
www.meals.com/Index/Index.aspx
home.ivillage.com/cooking/topics/0,,4thn,00.html
www.chefmom.com
www.onearmedcook.com/index.htm
www.busycooks.about.com/cs/beginningcooks/index.htm
www.bhg.com/bhg/category.jhtml?catref=C54
www.reluctantgourmet.com/basics.htm
www.pamperedchef.com

Crock Pot Cooking
www.crockpot.com/recipes.html
crockpot.allrecipes.com
southernfood.about.com/library/crock/blcpidx.htm
crockpot.cdkitchen.com/recipes

Recipes
Obviously, there are thousands upon thousands of recipe sites out there. I have chosen to list 5 sites that have simple to make meals that families will enjoy.

www.everydaycook.com

www.allrecipes.com

www.campbellkitchen.com

www.meals.com

www.rushhourcook.com

Money Resources

www.frugal-families.com

www.frugalmom.net

www.miserlymoms.com

www.mommysavers.com

www.stretcher.com

Work at Home Resources

www.Bizymoms.com

www.WAHM.com

www.mompreneursonline.com

www.webmomz.com

www.hbwm.com

www.internetbasedmoms.com

www.mymommybiz.com

www.moneymakingmommy.com

www.momsbusinessmagazine.com

Acknowledgements

Writing a book as a mom is a very arduous task. Without the help of many different people in my life, I never would have accomplished this feat.

First and foremost, I want to thank my wonderful husband. Without his encouragement, support and constant reassurance, this book would have never been written. I will never forget how much you helped me with this process. I am very lucky to be married to a guy like you. You mean the world to me.

Second, I would like to thank my publisher Nancy Cleary for believing in my idea and Linda Sharp for her wonderful editing skills.

I should also thank my kids for not causing too much damage to the house or to each other while my eyes were glued to the computer screen while putting this book together. I also want to thank them for putting up with my "Domestically Challenged-ness" on a daily basis. I love you guys.

A special thanks to my writing buddies Joyce Anthony and Jenn Satterwhite. Thanks for the words of encouragement when I needed them most.

To all the moms who are trying to get used to the idea of being an at home mom, I hope you find something that makes your job a little bit easier. If nothing else, always keep in mind that whatever goof you may think you have made, I'm sure I have topped it.

Wyatt-MacKenzie Publishing, Inc
WyMacPublishing.com

CPSIA information can be obtained
at www.ICGtesting.com
Printed in the USA
BVOW08s1434130517
484036BV00008B/97/P